Readings: A New Biblical Commentary

General Editor
John Jarick

1 CHRONICLES

1 CHRONICLES

John Jarick

SHEFFIELD ACADEMIC PRESS
A Continuum imprint
LONDON • NEW YORK

Copyright © 2002 Sheffield Academic Press
A Continuum imprint

Published by
Sheffield Academic Press Ltd
The Tower Building, 11 York Road, London SE1 7NX
370 Lexington Avenue, New York, NY 10017-6550

www.continuumbooks.com

British Library Cataloguing-in-Publication Data
A catalogue record for this book is available from the British Library

Typeset by Sheffield Academic Press
Printed on acid-free paper in Great Britain by MPG Books Ltd, Bodmin, Cornwall

ISBN   0-8264-6201-4 (hardback)
       0-8264-6202-2 (paperback)

Contents

Preface

This reading of 1 Chronicles has been some time in the making, and I am tempted to name the volume 'Jabez', taking my cue from that patriarch's mother, who bestowed such a name upon her son 'because I bore him in pain' (1 Chron. 4.9). But just as that honourable woman was mistaken in her etymology, so too it would be inaccurate to claim that the process of producing this work has been entirely painful. In fact, when busy schedules have allowed progress to be made on the project, it has been an enthralling task. These ancient Chronicles, admittedly not among many people's favourite reading matter, are more entertaining than some have realized, but also more disturbing than they might at first glance appear to be. I hope that I have done justice to both aspects in this volume.

A number of sections of this work began their life in the form of lectures delivered to the 'Old Testament Texts' class at the University of Surrey, Roehampton, and I also benefited from working through segments of the Hebrew text of Chronicles with the 'Hebrew Readings' class at the same institution. I wish to thank all the Roehampton students who shared the journey with me, especially Parveen Teji (who transferred the lectures from tape to type) and Angela Thomas (who contributed research to the section on the genealogical material).

The initial essay in the section 'Adam to Anani' began its life in the form of a paper delivered to the 17th Congress of the International Organization for the Study of the Old Testament at the University of Basel in August 2001, and is also appearing in a somewhat different form as 'The Implications of LXX 1 Chronicles 3.21 for King David's Place in the Chronicles Timeline' in M.F.J. Baasten and W.T. van Peursen (eds.), *Hamlet on a Hill* (Leuven: Peeters, forthcoming).

I am grateful to David Clines of Sheffield Academic Press for inviting me to contribute a reading of Chronicles to the *Readings* series (and indeed also for subsequently inviting me to act as General Editor for the series), and I am equally grateful to Duncan Burns for his fine copy-editing in bringing the work to publication (as well as for his assistance with 'genealogical' research earlier in the project). At the end, I could not have wished for a more conducive venue in which to complete my manuscript than St Stephen's House, and so I thank that community—and the wider circle of colleagues in Oxford—for taking me in.

Oxford
October 2002

Introduction

Reading Chronicles First

Some people evidently felt that, of all the scriptures of Israel, the book of Chronicles should be read last. We might call those people 'The Codex Compilers of the Hebrew Bible', since such tradents decided that Chronicles should be bound in at the very end of the canonical collection. There is no shame in being last, and indeed it can be seen as a privileged position to have been given the final word among all the words of Scripture. The ultimate matter in the whole Hebrew Bible arranged in this way is the ultimate matter of Chronicles, namely the prospect of a new beginning, the potentially bright future that awaits because God is at work creating a new opportunity. 'Whoever is among you of all [Yahweh's] people, may their god Yahweh be with them! Let them go up [to Jerusalem]!' (2 Chron. 36.23). In a Bible with such an ending, Chronicles may claim to be the climax and perhaps even the interpretive key to the whole. Yet readers may be inclined, when encountering this book after its canonical bedfellows, to see it as a somewhat superfluous recapping of what has already been told in the pages that precede it.

Other people apparently thought that Chronicles should be read immediately after Samuel and Kings. We might call those people 'The Codex Compilers of the Greek Bible', since such tradents decided that Chronicles should be bound in as a kind of appendix to the books of the Kingdoms. Perhaps there is no shame in being labelled *Paraleipomenon*, 'Omitted Things', the things that had not fitted in to the earlier books. A supplement to the books of the Kingdoms with extra information about the kingdom of Judah can take an honoured place in the canonical collection, sitting appropriately enough alongside the other apparently historical writings. Yet readers may be inclined, when encountering this book after the narratives of Samuel and Kings, to see it as very much a 'secondary history' not particularly compatible with the 'primary history' that precedes it.

But I wonder what would have been thought of such codicial arrangements by the people responsible for creating the scroll of Chronicles in the first place, had they lived to see their work being bound in with other writings. We might call those people 'The Annalists', since the work they produced, entitled in Hebrew *divrey hayyamim*, can be rendered 'The Annals' (more literally 'an account of the days' rather than 'of the years', but the slight paraphrase is fully justifiable in view of the content of the work). The rendering of the title as 'Chronicles'—following a suggestion of the Latin biblical scholar Jerome and generally used in English biblical studies—is perfectly fine, but it is worth noting that, when the expression occurs within the work itself, many modern English translations do in fact render it as 'the Annals', such as the New Revised Standard Version's 'the Annals of King David' for *divrey hay-yamim lammelek david* (in 1 Chron. 27.24).

Thus 'The Annals' will be employed in this reading of the document that is more traditionally known as 'Chronicles'. So too this study will not speak of 'the Chronicler' as the putative author of the work, as is the general fashion among biblical scholars, but will rather speak of 'the Annalists'. In using this designation, it is hoped that two interpretive aspects will be suggested which may not be so ably signified by the designation 'the Chronicler'.

Primarily I wish to signal that the book we have access to is not the product of a single author, not even in terms of that historical-critical model which postulates an original Chronicler upon whose foundation various levitical additions were laid or sundry priestly revisions were made. I rather think that the scroll from the first was the product of a collective enterprise of assembling, sifting, and refining certain Jerusalemite traditions; that is to say, that a community or guild of tradents was responsible for the composition of these Annals. I could of course speak of 'the Chroniclers' if the collective aspect of authorship was all that I wanted to imply for this work, but I am also attracted to the homonymous relationship between the word 'Annalists' (designating a school of chronographers) and the word 'Analysts' (designating professionals or others who apply analytical skills to their tasks). The people responsible for telling the story of the kingdom of Judah through the pages of these Annals had exactingly analyzed the events of the years under their scrutiny, and they put forward an account which scrupulously insisted on their line of analysis. This is an account which seeks to avoid any loose ends in the tale, and which brooks no alternative vision of the 'how' and the 'why' of it all. It does not sit easily alongside competing narratives. It demands to be read first, or indeed to be the only scroll consulted on matters concerning the House of David.

We of course have ready access to those other scrolls purporting to tell of matters concerning the House of David and various rival houses, namely the books of Samuel and Kings, since we have inherited the legacy of the Codex Compilers. What the Annalists apparently sought to achieve looks to have been undermined by the later community of faith in its decision to preserve two competing versions of the events of those years. The Annalists created what to their minds should have stood *[handwritten marginal note: ? but assumes audience knows tradition knows tradition (in S-K)]*

unrivalled among the Judean community as the definitive account of the nation's monarchical era, but there for all the world to see is its rival, the account in Samuel and Kings, superciliously agreeing with the Annals at times, stridently contradicting them at other times, and often enough diverting readers with tales of a northern kind, all the while winning the debate in certain quarters about what really happened and what it might have meant.

Yet Chronicles can still be read 'first', as it were. We can set aside the scrolls of Samuel and Kings, and contemplate Chronicles without their interference. I don't say that these Annals ought to be contemplated without reference to any other ancient Hebrew documentation; since the Annalists present in their opening chapters a kaleidoscope of figures from the ancestral ages, and since they also seem to take as read a certain amount of Mosaic material, I do not suppose that they necessarily wished to replace or suppress writings which were concerned with other matters than specifically the events and protagonists of the monarchical period. But when it comes to the telling of the tale of the House of David, I imagine that the Annalists would indeed have wished for no rival storytellers.

Accordingly, the commentary which follows will seek to discover what may be heard if one listens single-mindedly to the Annalists' account, tuning out the competing stories about David and his dynasty that might otherwise vie for our attention. At first, as we inspect the parade of ancestral figures in the opening chapters of the Annals, we will naturally call to mind the ancient legends surrounding the patriarchs of Israel to be found in such venerable documents as the book of Genesis, but, once we come to 'the Annals of King David' as such, any rival accounts of his life and deeds—as represented in the books of Samuel and Kings—form no part of the reading.

Reading First Chronicles

Exactly what document is being read here? The term 'Annals' alongside 'the book of Chronicles' and at the same time the designations '1 Chronicles' and '2 Chronicles' as two separate 'books' may seem to cloud the issue. But the matter is simple enough. The Hebrew scroll of Chronicles is a single document, beginning with the name of the primeval human 'Adam' (1 Chron. 1.1) and ending with the decree of the Persian king Cyrus (2 Chron. 36.23); it is this complete Hebrew document that forms the basis of this study, and so the present volume does not treat '1 Chronicles' as a book separate from '2 Chronicles' but rather understands them as one continuous work. But the ancient Greek translators found it useful—not least because their language in written form takes up more space on a scroll than does the Hebrew script—to divide the work into two, ending the first half of the account at the end of the reign of King David (1 Chron. 29.30) and beginning a second half with the story of King Solomon (2 Chron. 1.1); this divide has remained a useful practical device, and so the present volume takes the story up to the end of David's reign and will be followed by a second volume exploring beyond that point.

Although the Hebrew document is in view, this study is presented in English, and many readers will have a standard English text alongside them. Since the New Revised Standard Version (hereafter NRSV) is now a widely used text, the cadences of that version have been generally accepted in these pages, but not entirely. For one thing, the NRSV's designations for divinity have not been accepted here; where English readers may be used to seeing such expressions as 'the LORD your God said to you' (1 Chron. 11.2) or 'David inquired of God' (14.10), in these pages they will see 'your god Yahweh said to you' and 'David inquired of the deity', which arguably render the Hebrew more accurately though less piously than the traditional translations. In addition to the question of divine names and designations, there are also a number of other specific occasions where I have preferred an alternative rendering to that chosen by the NRSV panel, but in such individual cases attention is drawn to the difference between my rendering and the wording of the standard translation.

Some readings of Chronicles divide the work into segments that stem from 'the Chronicler' and other segments that stem from one or another source-document utilized by 'the Chronicler' and yet further segments that have been added to the work after the time of 'the Chronicler' by one or another tradent. It should be evident from what was said earlier that the present reading is not interested in such theorization, but is only concerned with the work of 'the Annalists' as we find it. But equally it might be noted in this context that it is the work indicated above—the document stretching from the name of Adam to the decree of Cyrus—that is the book in view here, and no special attachment is made to the scroll of Ezra–Nehemiah, which some interpreters (though fewer nowadays than used to be the case) take as part of the work of 'the Chronicler'.

So too the present study does not theorize about precisely when the scroll was written, or which other now-biblical scrolls were in existence at the time (references to other 'canonical' writings in the comments below should not be taken as implying that the Annalists knew those precise documents). Some of the traditions represented within the Annals may be very old ones indeed, while others may have been rather freshly devised by the compilers themselves. Perhaps there were other written accounts in existence by the time the Annalists set about their task, or perhaps they were working at more or less the same time as various teams of chroniclers were putting together their own accounts. They may have copied certain matters from the scrolls of Samuel and Kings, or both they and the compilers of Samuel and Kings may have copied certain matters from another scroll; it might even be that the Samuel–Kings scribes made some use of these Annals. Since our task is to read the Annals in their own right as a coherent piece of literature with its own life, we need not join such endless debates.

All that can be said with certainty about the date of composition of *date* these Annals is that they were not compiled in their present form before the Persian conquest of Babylon (alluded to at the end of 2 Chronicles, and already assumed in the post-exilic settlers list in 1 Chron. 9), and accordingly that the work could not have been completed before the late sixth century BCE. It is probably significantly later than that, and if the genealogy of Davidic descendants in 1 Chronicles 3 is anything to go by *[? They only go that far in the LXX]* then the final touches to the document were not made until the late third century BCE. However, since there seem to be other considerations than strictly historical ones on the part of the Annalists in setting out the number of generations that they do in their list of the direct line of descent from David (see the comments in the 'Adam to Anani' section below), no firm grounds for dating the composition can be derived from such 'data'.

From whatever distance in time, the Annalists are looking back to a mythical past. Theirs is a 'book of beginnings'. By starting out with Adam and the generations that were believed to have descended from him, they allude to the very beginnings of humankind and in turn to the beginnings of the great divisions of peoples in the known world and the beginnings of the Israelite people itself. By devoting an inordinate amount of text to their story of King David as founder of the kingdom of Israel and planner of the temple of Yahweh, and (in 2 Chronicles) to their story of the building and dedication of the temple by King Solomon, they show that they are most interested in getting across a certain view of the beginnings of the regal and religious system they advocate. And by drawing the Annals to a close with the invitation from the Persian king for people to 'go up', they end with a new beginning—and an implied challenge for their community, to act in accordance with the way the Annalists envisaged things to have been constituted in the earlier beginning of the 'kingdom of Yahweh'.

And here lies a rather uncomfortable aspect of the Annalists' agenda: if *† quite* anyone might have been thinking that they wanted to establish Israelite or Judean practice in some other way, or might have felt that a strict system in political and religious life of men receiving the mantle of royal or priestly office from their fathers is not necessarily the best way forward, the message of the Annalists is that the traditions are sacrosanct, even part of the divine cosmic plan, set up by the incomparably great David himself with the full blessing of heaven, right from the beginning of the Israelite kingdom. Only absolute commitment to a system instituted by an absolute monarch can bring about a perfect society, seems to be the underlying theme running through the columns of this scroll.

Of course it is only one group's telling of the story, and is 'history'-telling only of a certain propagandistic kind. There may be some particular historical groundedness to parts of the tale, but in many respects these Annals have the character of fantasy literature. They create an imaginary world in which things happen just so, and in which almost all the 'loose ends' are tied together in a highly systematic way. This is storytelling with the didactic purpose of inculcating a particular ideology, bombarding the reader with a kaleidoscopic procession of heroes and villains and presenting a frontierland of danger and opportunity. There is considerable artistry in the telling of the tale (even including at times a distinctly musical language), yet that does not entirely mask the dark underbelly of the writing (with its persistent note of conformity to the system advocated by the Annalists). While appreciating the artistry of the ancient tradents, and enjoying many aspects of the literary world of the text, a modern reader cannot entirely put aside the notions that one brings to a reading of the text from a real world that has experienced the horrors of totalitarianism and fundamentalism.

Thus there is something decidedly uncomfortable, yet also fascinating, in handling a scroll that seems to claim for itself the distinction of being the authoritative account of how things were and how they should be. But it is precisely such a scroll that we are encountering when we read 'The Annals'. Let us begin, then, with the first instalment: '1 Chronicles'.

Adam to Anani
(1 Chronicles 1–9)

1 Chronicles 1–9:
David's Generation in its Context

The Annals begin with a parade of names: 'Adam' launches the series and is followed in immediate succession by a line of descent that lists 'Seth, Enosh, Kenan, Mahalalel' and so on; the generations from the beginning of time march across the page. This is not everyone's idea of riveting reading, but there is method among the masses of names, with the procession of worthies moving more slowly as the Annalists cast some sideways glances at the spreading branches of the human family and then more particularly as they focus in on the sons of Israel, and within the sons of Israel on the sons of Judah, and within the sons of Judah on the house of David.

As we approach that decisive juncture, the figures linger somewhat longer, with the more elongated formulation of 'Nahshon, prince of the sons of Judah; and Nahshon became the father of Salma, and Salma became the father of Boaz, and Boaz became the father of Obed, and Obed became the father of Jesse' (2.10-12), and then 'Jesse became the father of...' a full seven sons and two daughters, with David listed as the seventh and ultimate son (2.15). After an intermission, the list lingers on an itemized tally of David's 19 sons from seven wives (3.1-9), and then the procession of state of the Davidic dynasty moves across the page, with the royal line of descent through 'the son of Solomon, Rehoboam; Abijah, his son; Asa, his son; Jehoshaphat, his son' (3.10), and so on down the line again in uninterrupted generational sequence, until we come to Josiah, more than one of whose sons sits on the throne in Jerusalem, and then to Jeconiah, 'the captive' (v. 17).

But Jeconiah's captivity does not bring an end to the Davidic line, for he too has a son, indeed a full complement of seven sons (vv. 17-18), and so the procession starts up again, not now of reigning monarchs but of potential kings, each one in his turn a possible candidate to take his rightful place on a refounded throne in Jerusalem. Unfortunately their steps become a little tangled, and some confusion is to be seen in the ranks. Untidiness creeps into an otherwise well-ordered procession at the point of 3.21. 'And the son of Hananiah, Pelatiah' reads well enough, but then 'and Jeshaiah' might suggest that 'son' in the singular was an error. Yet a similar listing of more than one son despite the introductory 'son' in the singular had occurred in the previous generation (v. 19), and the overall display seemed not to be too badly affected by that small infelicity. However, on this occasion matters are compounded by what follows, for the text appears to speak of 'sons of Rephaiah, sons of Arnan, sons of Obadiah, [and] sons of Shecaniah' (v. 21).

Perhaps we are meant to think of these four individuals named here as brothers of the same generation as the previous two brothers, each of the brothers becoming the father of a flourishing house. But the formulation in the received Hebrew text at this point is not in keeping with the rest of the dynastic chart, and so the reading of the venerable Greek, Syriac and Latin versions (together with certain other Hebrew manuscripts) is to be preferred, namely that the son of Hananiah is Pelatiah, who is followed in generational sequence by 'Jeshaiah, his son; Rephaiah, his son; Arnan, his son' and so on. This is in keeping with the formulation earlier in the dynastic chart, where we read (in v. 10) of the descendants of Solomon: 'Rehoboam; Abijah, his son; Asa, his son; Jehoshaphat, his son' and so on down the line. Such a sequence of 'his son' (*beno* in Hebrew, as in v. 10) makes better sense than a sequence of 'sons of' (*beney* in Hebrew, as in the mainstream text of v. 21). It is easy to see how the scribal slip to be found in the mainstream text of v. 21 occurred—it is a simple and all too common confusion between the Hebrew letters *vav* and *yod*—and it is just as easily corrected.

But is there any particular consequence in whether the Annalists intended to have pass by us in this verse just one generation in a list of six brothers or in fact six succeeding generations in a sequence of father and son and grandson and so on? Well, a rather interesting aspect emerges here: if we make the reading I have suggested, somewhat against the received Hebrew text but in full accordance with the other ancient versions, then the entire number of generations from David to his last-named descendant, Anani (v. 24), is 32, exactly the same number as the generations from Adam to Jesse.

Perhaps this is a coincidence, or perhaps the 'corrected' reading of the problematic verse is misplaced, but if it is not a mistaken piece of text-critical hocus-pocus then it does suggest that the Annalists were able to devise a rather clever balance to their generational matrix, although by not making it explicit they were unable to prevent a simple confusion between *vav* and *yod* from masking their achievement. And that achievement seems to have <u>been a calculated placement of David at the centre of the whole span of human history</u> as sketched by the Annalists in their genealogical record. Adam to Jesse equals 32 generations; David to Anani equals 32 generations. What could be neater?

Now there may be more here than a cleverness on the part of the Annalists in presenting a finely balanced 'before David' and 'after David' system. If the 'before David' span of generations had been 32, and then the incomparable man arose, what might happen after a further 32 generations? The genealogical schematization in the Annals might have tantalizingly invited their first readers, presumably members of that second thirty-second generation, to speculate on whether a 'new David' could be destined to arise in their generation. A seemingly innocuous list of names can, therefore, have considerable significance in the interpretation of these Annals.

It is true to say that the Annalists do not flag up in their work an overt vision of a renewed kingdom of Judah with a prince from the house of David reigning again on the throne in Jerusalem, and so readers may debate whether such a hope is at all nourished by this book, beyond the evident possibilities inherent in the dynastic oracle of 1 Chronicles 17. Perhaps the idealized picture of David presented in the body of the work (1 Chron. 10–29), or the sketching of certain of his descendants like Hezekiah as a kind of *David redivivus* (2 Chron. 29–32), or the closing challenge to 'whoever is among you of all [Yahweh's] people…let them go up!' (2 Chron. 36.23), are indications that some such hope was cherished. But perhaps even more so, the Annalists' crafting of genealogical lists which just so happen to place their generation at a mark on the chronological grid equal to the generation of yore that had witnessed the rise of the great David himself, indicates a considerable yearning for a New David.

In any event the matching 32 generations certainly look like more than simply a numerical quirk, since elsewhere in their work the Annalists demonstrate that they are rather interested in numbers and measurements, and in weighing up one accounting against another. Witness for example in the story concerning David's tabulation of his troops in 1 Chronicles 21 that the census figures compute at a threefold increase in the numbers of fighting men in Israel during his reign, and that the king is presented with a threefold choice of punishment for his census, each punishment involving a threefold period of time: one lasting for three years, one lasting for three months, and one lasting for three days, which neatly stand in reverse to the three days of blessings in ch. 12 (v. 39), the three months of blessings in ch. 13 (v. 14), and the three years of blessings in 2 Chronicles 11 (v. 17). Or we might note too that in the same account David pays 600 shekels for the temple site. Bearing in mind that Exodus 30.12-14 stipulates that 'When you take a census of the Israelites to register them, at registration all of them shall give a ransom [of half a shekel] for their lives to Yahweh, so that no plague may come upon them for being registered', then the price that David pays for the newly designated sacred site at the point where the census-provoked plague has come to a standstill may be interpreted as a kind of ransom for the lives of his people. 600 shekels are 1200 half-shekels, representing a hundredfold ransom for each of the twelve tribes of Israel, and thus reflecting Joab's reference at the beginning of that particular episode to a hyperbolic hundredfold increase of Yahweh's people.

So then, if this group of tradents has set out a scheme of generations in which 'Adam to Jesse' equals 'David to Anani', that seems too neat an arrangement to be dismissed as meaningless in their scheme of things. It is said that in every generation there are some who believe that a long-destined day is at last at hand. It would seem that among the Annalists such a belief was indeed to be found. One can imagine that they sustained themselves at least with the statistical possibility, and perhaps even with the fervent hope, that their generation stood on the cusp of significant renewal in their nation's destiny. A fresh turning of the age could be just one birth away, a tantalizing prospect suggested in the number of generations that had passed before the time of the accounting in their book of Annals.

But whatever they believed the future to hold, it is clear that the Annalists had a very systematic view of the past. In these genealogical lists they allow themselves to be distracted marginally from the central line that holds their interest, in order to give some shape to the surrounding peoples (in ch. 1) and more particularly to set out the shape of the Israelite tribes as they envisaged them (in chs. 2–9), most especially the tribes of Judah (2.3–4.23) and Levi (6.1–7.81) as the 'regal' and 'priestly' groups centred on Jerusalem. Yet even as branches spread out from the centre, in each generation there remains a focus. The idea at work here is put later into the mouth of David himself (in 28.4-5): 'Yahweh, the god of Israel, chose me from all my ancestral house to be king over Israel forever; for he chose Judah as leader, and in the house of Judah my father's house, and among my father's sons he took delight in making me king over all Israel; and of all my sons, for Yahweh has given me many, he has chosen my son Solomon to sit upon the throne of the kingdom of Yahweh over Israel.'

Thus we can trace—as presented in the following pages—a continuous central line through the full 64 generations of Annalistic genealogies, with various significant sidelines branching off in certain generations, but only one line going the distance. The line sets out from Adam and leads through the kaleidoscope of figures inexorably to David, and beyond David it leads on to the generation that culminates in Anani.

● **Adam** ————————————————————————————————

The parade of the generations begins with the eponymous 'man' (*adam* in Hebrew) from which all humankind is descended (1.1). This designation for humanity is employed a number of times in the Annals, in such phrases as 'You regard me as a person (*adam*) of high rank' (17.17) and 'Let me fall into the hand of Yahweh, for his mercy is very great, but let me not fall into human hands' (literally, 'into the hand of *adam*', 21.13), but there are no further references to the initial Adam as such; his role in the Annals is simply to stand at the beginning. A more fleshed-out account of how the ancient Hebrews imagined things to have begun is supplied in the book of Genesis, where we read: 'In the day that the god Yahweh made the earth and the heavens, when no plant of the field was yet in the earth and no herb of the field had yet sprung up—for the god Yahweh had not caused it to rain upon the earth, and there was no one to till the ground; but a stream would rise from the earth, and water the whole face of the ground—then the god Yahweh formed man (*adam*) from the dust of the ground, and breathed into his nostrils the breath of life; and the man became a living being' (Genesis 2.4-7). But it ends in tears: 'And to Adam he said, "Because you have listened to the voice of your wife, and have eaten of the tree about which I commanded you, 'You shall not eat of it', cursed is the ground because of you; in toil you shall eat of it all the days of your life; thorns and thistles it shall bring forth for you; and you shall eat the plants of the field. By the sweat of your face you shall eat bread until you return to the ground, for out of it you were taken; you are dust, and to dust you shall return"' (Genesis 3.17-19).

● Seth

The inheritor of the primeval legacy is just a name in the
Annals, though Genesis has an eye to the meaning of that
name, telling of how the first mother 'bore a son, and named
him Seth, for she said, "God has sethed/appointed for me
another child instead of Abel, because Cain killed him"'
(Genesis 4.25). This 'Appointed One' is said to have 'lived for
105 years [when] he became the father of Enosh', and further
to have 'lived after the birth of Enosh for 807 years, and [to
have] had other sons and daughters; thus all the days of Seth
were 912 years, and he died' (Genesis 5.6-8). The writers of
Genesis do not disclose the age at the birth of Enosh or any
other details regarding Seth's wife, but the reference to
Adam's (and Eve's) 'other sons and daughters' (5.4) is suggestive of where the storytellers imagined Seth would have had
to have looked for a partner (indeed the retelling of the story
in the book of *Jubilees* fleshed out such a suggestion by
informing readers of that version of events that 'Seth took
Azura, his sister, as a wife' [*Jubilees* 4.11]). However, the Annalists have no interest in retelling any stories about Seth or
his brothers and sisters, but only in listing Seth in the second-
generation position. Similarly, they do not allow themselves
to be distracted, as Genesis does (in Genesis 4.17-22), into
providing a genealogical record of the descendants of Seth's
older brother Cain; since all human lines of descent apart
from that of Seth to Noah were wiped out in the great flood
(Genesis 7.23), only the line represented by Seth is relevant
in the Annalists' scheme of things.

• Enosh

The third man in the sequence of generations carries, like the first man Adam, a generic name for 'man, human being' (the word is used in that sense in, for example, Deuteronomy 32.26: 'blot out the memory of them from Enosh/human-kind'), and thus serves as a further symbolic ancestor of all humanity. The individual so named is the subject of a short 'biography' in the book of Genesis: 'When Enosh had lived for 90 years, he became the father of Kenan; Enosh lived after the birth of Kenan for 815 years, and had other sons and daughters; thus all the days of Enosh were 905 years, and he died' (Genesis 5.9-11). The alternative version in the book of *Jubilees* puts it this way: 'In the seventh "jubilee" [i.e. in the seventh 49-year period of the earth as envisaged by the writers of *Jubilees*], in the third "week" [i.e. in the third seven-year period within that "jubilee"], Enosh took Noam, his sister, as a wife, and she bore a son for him in the third year of the fifth "week", and he named him Kenan' (*Jubilees* 4.13). Genesis also includes—and *Jubilees* copies in a fashion—a curious note that at the time of Enosh's own birth 'people began to invoke the name of Yahweh' (Genesis 4.26)—curious because Eve was earlier pictured as having invoked precisely that divine name at the birth of her firstborn (Genesis 4.1: 'I have produced a man with the help of Yahweh') and also because Moses was later told that previous generations had not known the deity by that name (Exodus 6.3: 'I am Yahweh. I appeared to Abraham, Isaac and Jacob as "El Shaddai", but by my name "Yahweh" I did not make myself known to them').

● **Kenan**

The fourth generation of humanity is represented solely by the figure of Kenan (1.2). This name has to do with productivity or acquisition, and so may be thought to symbolize the growth of the human population or the development of various human activities in those primeval days. The book of Genesis actually gives the explanation of the name in its story of the first procreated human, namely Cain (whose name in Hebrew, *kayin*, is a variation on *kenan*, the two of them resonating with the verb *kanah*, 'to acquire' or 'to buy'), when it says: 'Now the man knew his wife Eve, and she conceived and bore Cain, saying, "I have produced (*kanah*) a man with the help of Yahweh"' (Genesis 4.1). The explanation is not repeated when it comes to reporting that 'when Enosh had lived for 90 years, he became the father of Kenan' (Genesis 5.9), followed by some brief 'statistics' regarding Kenan's own life: 'When Kenan had lived for 70 years, he became the father of Mahalalel; Kenan lived after the birth of Mahalalel for 840 years, and had other sons and daughters; thus all the days of Kenan were 910 years, and he died' (Genesis 5.12-14). The alternative version in the book of *Jubilees* puts it this way: 'At the end of the eighth "jubilee", Kenan took for himself a wife, Mualeleth, his sister, and she bore a son for him in the ninth "jubilee", in the first "week", in the third year, and he called him Mahalalel' (*Jubilees* 4.14).

● **Mahalalel**

The fifth generation of humanity is represented solely by the figure of Mahalalel (1.2). Readers might note the *halal* component of the name (from the verb *hillel*), which has to do with singing the praises of someone, in this case those of the deity El (or 'God' per se)—many will be familiar with the expression *halleluyah* or 'praise Yah[weh]!' in the book of Psalms (such as at the beginning and again at the end of each of Psalms 146– 150). But the ancient storytellers do not dwell on such a matter in relation to Mahalalel. Genesis simply gives the following dry account of the man: 'When Mahalalel had lived for 65 years, he became the father of Jared; Mahalalel lived after the birth of Jared for 830 years, and had other sons and daughters; thus all the days of Mahalalel were 895 years, and he died' (Genesis 5.15-17). The alternative version in the book of *Jubilees* puts it this way: 'In the second "week" of the tenth "jubilee", Mahalalel took for himself a wife, Dinah, the daughter of Barakiel, the daughter of his father's brother, and she bore a son for him in the third "week", in the sixth year, and he called him Jared because in his days the angels of Yahweh, who were called Watchers, came down to the earth in order to teach mortals, and perform judgment and uprightness upon the earth' (*Jubilees* 4.15). Thus nothing is ventured about why Kenan might have named his son 'Mahalalel', but a considerable interest is shown in the name that Mahalalel bestows upon his own son, who now follows in the primeval succession.

● Jared

The sixth generation of humanity is represented solely by the figure of Jared (1.2). In the book of *Jubilees* we read that his father Mahalalel 'called him Jared because in his days the angels of Yahweh, who were called Watchers, came down to the earth in order to teach mortals, and perform judgment and uprightness upon the earth. In the eleventh "jubilee", in the fourth "week", Jared took for himself a wife, and her name was Baraka, the daughter of Rasuyal, the daughter of his father's brother, and she bore a son for him in the fifth "week", in the fourth year, and he called him Enoch' (*Jubilees* 4.15-16). The verb *yarad*, 'to go down' or 'to descend', is a very common one in Hebrew, and so the name 'Jared' might have been linked with any sort of descent, such as a movement of population from hunting grounds in the hill country to the agricultural settlements in the plains, but the writers of *Jubilees* prefer to connect it with an ancient legend about heavenly beings descending upon the earth. The compilers of Genesis make no comment upon the name 'Jared', but they do have their own version of such a descent in prehistoric times: 'When people began to multiply on the face of the ground, and daughters were born to them, the divine beings saw that they were fair, and they took wives for themselves of all that they chose. Then Yahweh said, "My spirit shall not abide in mortals forever, for they are flesh; their days shall be 120 years"' (Genesis 6.1-3). But this 120-year limit was not seen as being enforced already in Jared's day, since we are told that 'when Jared had lived for 162 years, he became the father of Enoch; Jared lived after the birth of Enoch for 800 years, and had other sons and daughters; thus all the days of Jared were 962 years, and he died' (Genesis 5.18-20).

• Enoch

The seventh generation of humanity is represented solely by the figure of Enoch (1.3). The book of Genesis expresses his 'biography' in the following way: 'When Enoch had lived for 65 years, he became the father of Methuselah; Enoch walked with the deity after the birth of Methuselah for 300 years, and had other sons and daughters; thus all the days of Enoch were 365 years. Enoch walked with the deity, then he was no more, because the deity took him' (Genesis 5.21-24). The unique phrasing here, with the twofold 'Enoch walked with the deity' and the final 'then he was no more, because the deity took him', speaks of a special individual, but Genesis says no more about him. It might have commented on his name, which has to do with the notion of 'training' (as in Proverbs 22.6: 'Enoch/train a child in the right way, and when he is old, he will not stray'), but it does not. *Jubilees*, on the other hand, has much to say on this theme: 'Enoch was the first who learned knowledge and writing and wisdom, from among mortals, from among those who were born upon earth, and who wrote in a book the signs of the heaven according to the order of their months, so that mortals might know the appointed times of the years according to their order, with respect to each of their months; he was the first who wrote a testimony and testified to mortals throughout the generations of the earth, and their "weeks" according to "Jubilees" he recounted, and the days of the years he made known, and the months he set in order, and the sabbaths of the years he recounted… In the twelfth "jubilee", in the seventh "week", Enoch took for himself a wife, and her name was Edni, the daughter of Danel, his father's brother, and in the sixth year of that "week" she bore a son for him, and he called him Methuselah' (*Jubilees* 4.17-20).

● Methuselah

The eighth generation of humanity is represented solely by
the figure of Methuselah (1.3). The statistics concerning him
in the book of Genesis are the most impressive of all the
primeval line, since we are told that 'when Methuselah had
lived for 187 years, he became the father of Lamech; Methuselah lived after the birth of Lamech for 782 years, and had
other sons and daughters; thus all the days of Methuselah
were 969 years, and he died' (Genesis 5.25-27). At very little
less than a full millennium, Methuselah is thus seen as the
longest living of any mortal in the Hebrew legends. His grandfather Jared, at 962 years, is not far behind him in this
achievement, but his father Enoch, at a mere 365 years, and
his son Lamech, at 777 years, are striplings in comparison.
The writers of *Jubilees*, with their scheme of human history
falling in a destined number of 'Jubilees' or 49-year periods,
have different calculations in mind, and the length of life of
the ancient worthies are not of particular interest to them, in
contrast to the year of birth for each new generation in the
overall timescale. Thus we read of Methuselah only the following: 'In the fourteenth "jubilee", in the third "week", in
the first year, Methuselah took for himself a wife, and her
name was Edna, daughter of Azrial, his father's brother, and
she bore a son for him, and he called him Lamech' (*Jubilees*
4.27). Why Methuselah was called 'Methuselah' is not commented upon by either *Jubilees* or Genesis, but the *selah* (in
Hebrew *shelach*) part of the name has to do with 'letting go'
or 'sending', so the whole may denote a man who travels to a
new place or who is skilful in throwing a weapon (sometimes
called a *shelach*, as in Joel 2.8).

• Lamech

The ninth generation of humanity is represented solely by the figure of Lamech (1.3). The statistics concerning him in the book of Genesis are as follows: 'When Lamech had lived for 182 years, he became the father of a son; he named him Noah, saying, "Out of the ground that Yahweh has cursed this one shall bring us relief from our work and from the toil of our hands". Lamech lived after the birth of Noah for 595 years, and had other sons and daughters; thus all the days of Lamech were 777 years, and he died' (Genesis 5.28-31). The alternative version in the book of *Jubilees* puts it this way: 'In the fifteenth "jubilee", in the third "week", Lamech took for himself a wife, and her name was Betenos, the daughter of Barakiil, the daughter of his father's brother, and in that "week" she bore a son for him, and he called him Noah, saying "This one will console me from my grief and from all of my labour and from the land which Yahweh cursed"' (*Jubilees* 4.28). Thus the name of Lamech's son is given an explanation by both Genesis and *Jubilees*, but the name of Lamech himself remains unexplained—and indeed this particular name, unlike the others around it in the primeval genealogy, is not clearly related to any Hebrew words known to us, so any meaning that it might have had for the ancient genealogists is no longer recoverable. Genesis does, however, record a story concerning a legendary Lamech (although it places it within the genealogy of Cain's descendants rather than Seth's): 'Lamech said to his wives, "Adah and Zillah, hear my voice; you wives of Lamech, listen to what I say: I have killed a man for wounding me, a young man for striking me; for Cain is avenged sevenfold, but Lamech seventy-seven-fold"' (Genesis 4.23-24).

● Noah

The tenth generation of humanity is represented solely by the figure of Noah (1.4). The book of Genesis has an explanation for his name, stating that his father Lamech 'named him Noah, saying, "Out of the ground that Yahweh has cursed this one shall bring us relief from our work and from the toil of our hands"' (Genesis 5.29). Although implying that the name 'Noah' means 'relief', it hardly seems to explain matters, but later in the story we read that 'Noah, a man of the soil, was the first to plant a vineyard' (9.20), so that is presumably the means by which he is able to bring relief 'out of the ground that Yahweh has cursed'. But Noah's main claim to fame in the ancient Hebrew stories is as 'a righteous man, blameless in his generation' (6.9), who was spared the divine punishment that came upon the world in the form of a great flood. The deity 'blotted out every living thing that was on the face of the ground, human beings and animals and creeping things and birds of the air; they were blotted out from the earth. Only Noah was left, and those that were with him in the ark' (7.23)—the latter being 'his sons, Shem and Ham and Japheth, and Noah's wife and the wives of his sons' plus 'every wild animal of every kind, and all domestic animals of every kind, and every creeping thing that creeps on the earth, and every bird of every kind...two and two of all flesh in which there was the breath of life' (7.13-16). After it all, the deity 'blessed Noah and his sons, and said to them, "Be fruitful and multiply, and fill the earth"' (9.1). The 'filling of the earth' then follows: 'The sons of Noah who went out of the ark were Shem, Ham and Japheth... These three were the sons of Noah, and from these the whole earth was peopled' (9.18-19).

- **Shem**

  The eleventh man to occupy the line of destiny is the first to be listed with a set of siblings, as the Annalists envisage the branching out of the earth's peoples from a previously common primeval ancestry. Shem—whose name indeed means 'name' (i.e. 'man of renown')—is listed in pole position in 1.4, but then waits for his brothers' branches to be briefly catalogued before his own genealogy, the Shemite (Semite) or eastern human branch of central interest to the Annalists, is mapped out in detail from 1.17 onwards.

- **Ham**

  The middle brother Ham—whose name means 'warm' or 'hot'—is regarded as the ancestor of the peoples of the warmer southern regions. The Hamites are catalogued into four main subgroups in 1.8: the Cushites (further catalogued in vv. 9-10), the Egyptians (said in vv. 11-12 to be the root of a number of peoples, including the Philistines, who will step forward again later in the Annals), the Putites (not further itemized), and the Canaanites (catalogued into eleven different branches in vv. 13-16).

- **Japheth**

  The junior member in this threefold division of the world's peoples is the ancestor of the northern-and-western branch of humanity, the Japhethites, who are catalogued into seven main subgroups in 1.5: the Gomerites (further catalogued into three different branches in v. 6) and the Javanites (catalogued into four different branches in v. 7), as well as the Magogites, Madaites, Tubalites, Meschechites and Tirasites (none of which are further itemized in these Annals). The name 'Japheth' has to do with 'spaciousness', a matter alluded to in Genesis 9.27.

- **Elam**

  The eponymous ancestor of the Elamites is given seniority among the peoples notionally descended from Shem (1.17).

- **Asshur**

  The eponymous ancestor of the mighty Asshurites (Assyrians) also outranks the ancestor of the Hebrew peoples.

- **Arpachshad**

  The twelfth man to occupy the line of destiny is at first glance almost hidden in his generation, but his line will emerge.

- **Lud**

  The eponymous ancestor of the Ludites (Lydians) is represented as a younger brother of the Hebrews' ancestor.

- **Aram**

  The eponymous ancestor of the Aramites (Arameans) is similarly pictured as closely related to the Hebrew peoples.

- **Uz**

  The eponymous ancestor of the Uzites of the eastern desert region also appears here as a son of Shem.

- **Hul**

  The eponymous ancestor of the Hulites is likewise associated with the Shemite (Semite) branch of humanity.

- **Gether**

  The eponymous ancestor of the Getherites comes in at the penultimate position among the sons of Shem.

- **Meshech**

  The 'eastern' Meshechites of 1.17 (in contrast to the 'northern' ones of 1.5) are listed among the descendants of Shem.

● Shelah

The thirteenth generation sees the figure of Shelah standing on the line of destiny (1.24). Again the reader might turn to Genesis for some brief sketching out of certain Hebrew traditions regarding such a legendary ancestor. In addition to saying that Shelah's father Arpachshad had been 35 years old when Shelah was born and had lived an additional 403 years after Shelah's birth (thus implying that he had lived for a grand total of 438 years), Genesis puts forward the following statistics for Shelah himself: 'When Shelah had lived for 30 years, he became the father of Eber; and Shelah lived after the birth of Eber for 403 years, and had other sons and daughters' (Genesis 11.14-15). The obvious implication—though in these postdiluvian generations the total figures are not set out—is that Shelah's lifespan was 433 years. In the alternative version in the book of *Jubilees*, an additional generation comes in between Arpachshad and Shelah: Arpachshad and his wife Rasueya have a son Cainan, and then Cainan and his wife Melka have a son Shelah; moreover, *Jubilees* relates that his father 'called him Shelah because he said, "I have certainly been sent out"' (*Jubilees* 8.1, 5). Then the following version of Shelah's 'biography' is put forward: 'In the fourth year [of the second "week" of the thirtieth "jubilee"], Shelah was born, and he grew up, and he took a wife, and her name was Muak, daughter of Kesed, his father's brother; [he took her] as a wife in the thirty-first "jubilee", in the fifth "week", in the first year, and she bore a son for him in its fifth year, and he called him Eber' (*Jubilees* 8.6).

● **Eber**

The fourteenth generation sees the figure of Eber—the eponymous ancestor of the Eberites (Hebrews)—standing on the
line of destiny (1.25). The statistics concerning him in the
book of Genesis are as follows: 'When Eber had lived for 34
years, he became the father of Peleg; and Eber lived after the
birth of Peleg for 430 years, and had other sons and daughters' (Genesis 11.16-17); his total lifespan is thus seen as
comprising 464 years. Genesis also tells us that 'to Eber were
born two sons: the name of the one was Peleg, for in his days
the earth was divided, and his brother's name was Joktan'
(Genesis 10.25, on which matter 1 Chron. 1.19 is in total
agreement). The alternative version in the book of *Jubilees*
puts it this way: 'Eber took a wife, and her name was Azurad,
daughter of Nebrod, in the thirty-second "jubilee", in the
seventh "week", in the third year, and in its sixth year she
bore a son for him, and he called him Peleg, because in the
days when he was born the sons of Noah began dividing up
the earth for themselves... And it came to pass at the beginning of the thirty-third "jubilee" that they divided the earth in
three parts, for Shem, Ham, and Japheth, according to the inheritance of each' (*Jubilees* 8.7-8, 10). The Hebrew peoples,
too, will receive an allotment in the world, all symbolized in
the name 'Peleg', yet curiously the name 'Eber' itself, although
it is the eponym for the Hebrews (Eberites), is not given any
significance by the storytellers. It presumably means 'a no-
mad' or 'one who lives beyond a boundary' (from the verb
avar, 'to pass from one side to another, to cross a boundary'),
and in that respect it is a perfect designation for 'Abraham the
Hebrew' (Genesis 14.13), who left his former home among
the Chaldeans to live in a new and distant land which became
the home of the Hebrew nation.

• Peleg

 The fifteenth man to occupy the line of destiny carries a name which symbolizes something of the concept at work at various stages of this parade of generations: 'the name of the [first son of Eber] was Peleg, for in his days the earth was peleged/divided' (1.19). Thus the distinct peoples of the world are emerging, and indeed Peleg himself can be seen as representing, in the very next generation after the eponymous Eber, a splitting of the Eberites (Hebrews) into two divisions: the Pelegites who will give rise in time to the Israelites themselves, and the Joktanite branch which will have its own destiny that lies largely outside the concerns of the Annalists. So too the Annalists show no interest in more detailed traditions associated with Peleg (unlike Genesis 11.18, which says that Peleg became a father at the age of 30 and lived a further 209 years after that, having 'other sons and daughters' in addition to Reu).

• Joktan

The junior branch of Eberites (Hebrews) are those peoples seen as descended from Joktan, whose name—though it is not commented upon by the Annalists, whose interest was rather in the other side of the peleging/dividing line—appears to designate one who is 'smaller' or 'younger' (from the Hebrew verb *katan*). Thirteen sub-groups are itemized by the Annalists as coming under the Joktanite umbrella, namely the peoples known as Almodad, Sheleph, Hazarmaveth, Jerah, Hadoram, Uzal, Diklah, Ebal, Abimael, Sheba, Ophir, Havilah, and Jobab (1.20-23). Some of these Hebrew relatives will later make guest appearances in the Israelite story (e.g. 'the gold of Ophir' in 29.4 and 'the queen of Sheba' in 2 Chron. 9.1— although the latter might be thought of as the Cushite Sheba of 1 Chron. 1.9).

● **Reu**

The sixteenth generation sees the figure of Reu standing on the line of destiny (1.25). The statistics concerning him in the book of Genesis are as follows: 'When Reu had lived for 32 years, he became the father of Serug; and Reu lived after the birth of Serug for 207 years, and had other sons and daughters' (Genesis 11.20-21); his total lifespan is thus seen as comprising 239 years. The alternative version in the book of *Jubilees* puts it this way: 'In the thirty-fifth "jubilee", in the third "week", in the first year, Reu took a wife, and her name was Ora, daughter of Ur, son of Kesed, and she bore a son for him, and he called him Seroh, in the seventh year of that "week" in that "jubilee"' (*Jubilees* 11.1). Neither text gives an explanation for the name 'Reu', but there are two possibilities, on account of the word being homonymous in Hebrew. One meaning of the homonym is 'friend' or 'companion', while the other is 'shepherd' or 'pastoralist'. Both meanings can work in the case of the longer name 'Reuel' to be found in the Annalists' lists (in the Esauite [Edomite] genealogy at 1 Chron. 1.35-37 and in the Benjaminite genealogy at 9.8), which can either mean 'El [the deity] is my friend/companion' or 'El is my shepherd'. The first possibility might resonate with an expression in the Annals concerning the deity's relationship with the greatest of the patriarchs ('Did you not, O our god, drive out the inhabitants of this land before your people Israel, and give it forever to the descendants of your friend Abraham?' [2 Chron. 20.7]), although the Hebrew word for 'friend' in that expression is not the one in view here. Closer to Reu's name is the title 'Rea/Friend of the King' seen in 1 Chron. 27.33. On the other hand, the use in the hymnic traditions of Israel of the expression 'Yahweh is my shepherd' (Psalm 23.1) might suggest that 'Reuel' is to be understood as 'El is my shepherd', and thus that 'Reu' is be understood as a shepherd.

● Serug

The seventeenth generation sees the figure of Serug standing on the line of destiny (1.26). The statistics concerning him in the book of Genesis are as follows: 'When Serug had lived for 30 years, he became the father of Nahor; and Serug lived after the birth of Nahor for 200 years, and had other sons and daughters' (Genesis 11.22-23); his total lifespan is thus seen as comprising 230 years. Much more is said about this character and his times in the book of *Jubilees*: when he was born his father 'called him Seroh', but then 'the sons of Noah began fighting in order to take captive and to kill each other, to pour human blood upon the earth, to eat blood, to build fortified cities and walls and towers, so that a man will be raised up over the people, to set up the first kingdoms to go to war, people against people and nation against nation and city against city, and everyone will act to do evil and to acquire weapons of battle and to teach their sons war, and they began to take captive a city and to sell male and female slaves...and they made for themselves molten images, and everyone worshipped the icon which they made for themselves as a molten image, and they began making graven images and polluted likenesses... Therefore he called the name of Seroh, "Serug", because everyone had turned back to commit all sin and transgression. And he grew up and dwelt in Ur of the Chaldeans near the father of his wife's mother, and he used to worship idols; and he took a wife in the thirty-sixth "jubilee", in the fifth "week", in the first year, and her name was Melka, daughter of Kaber, daughter of his father's brother, and she bore for him Nahor in the first year of that "week"' (*Jubilees* 11.1-8).

● **Nahor**

The eighteenth generation sees the figure of Nahor standing on the line of destiny (1.26). The statistics concerning him in the book of Genesis are as follows: 'When Nahor had lived for 29 years, he became the father of Terah; and Nahor lived after the birth of Terah for 119 years, and had other sons and daughters' (Genesis 11.24-25); his total lifespan is thus seen as comprising 148 years. The alternative version in the book of *Jubilees* says that Nahor 'dwelt in Ur among the Chaldeans, and his father taught him the researches of the Chaldeans in order to practise divination and astrology according to the signs of heaven; and in the thirty-seventh "jubilee", in the sixth "week", in the first year, he took a wife, and her name was Iyaska, daughter of Nestag of the Chaldeans, and she bore for him Terah in the seventh year of that "week"' (*Jubilees* 11.8-10). Discussion about the meaning of the name 'Nahor' is not entered into by the ancient storytellers, although it might have occasioned a tale or two had they wished, for it carries the meaning of 'snorting', as in the rhetorical flourish to be found in Job 39.19-22: 'Do you give the horse its might? Do you clothe its neck with mane? Do you make it leap like the locust? Its majestic nahoring/snorting is terrible. It paws violently, exults mightily; it goes out to meet the weapons. It laughs at fear, and is not dismayed; it does not turn back from the sword'. A similar image appears in Jeremiah 8.16: 'The nahoring/snorting of their horses is heard from Dan; at the sound of the neighing of their stallions the whole land quakes.' Thus the name of Nahor could have been the subject of a vignette like that concerning Nimrod, 'the first on earth to become a mighty warrior; he was a mighty hunter before Yahweh, and so it is said, "Like Nimrod a mighty hunter before Yahweh"' (Genesis 10.8-9, in part to be found also in 1 Chron. 1.10), but 'Nahor' stands without any accompanying tale in our texts.

• Terah

The nineteenth generation sees the figure of Terah standing on the line of destiny (1.26). The book of Genesis provides the following 'biography' of this character: 'When Terah had lived for 70 years, he became the father of Abram, Nahor, and Haran...and Haran was the father of Lot. Haran died before his father Terah in the land of his birth, in Ur of the Chaldeans... Terah took his son Abram and his grandson Lot son of Haran, and his daughter-in-law Sarai, his son Abram's wife, and they went out together from Ur of the Chaldeans to go into the land of Canaan; but when they came to Haran, they settled there. The days of Terah were 205 years; and Terah died in Haran' (Genesis 11.26-28, 31-32). His total lifespan is thus seen as comprising 275 years. The book of *Jubilees* tells a more elaborate story, including these details: 'In the thirty-ninth "jubilee", in the second "week", in the first year, Terah took a wife, and her name was Edna, daughter of Abram, daughter of his father's sister, and in the seventh year of that "week" she bore a son for him, and he called him Abram, after the name of his mother's father, because he died before his daughter conceived a son... And Terah went out of Ur of the Chaldeans, he and his sons, so that they might come into the land of Lebanon and into the land of Canaan, and he dwelt in Haran, and Abram dwelt with Terah, his father, in Haran for two "weeks" of years... And it came to pass in the seventh year of the sixth "week" that [Abram] spoke with his father and let him know that he was going from Haran to walk in the land of Canaan so that he might see it and return to him. And Terah, his father, said to him, "Go in peace; may the eternal god make straight your path and Yahweh be with you and protect you from all evil; may no mortal rule over you to do evil to you; go in peace"' (*Jubilees* 11.14-15; 12.15, 28-29).

● Abraham

The twentieth generation sees the figure of 'Abram, that is, Abraham' standing on the line of destiny (1.27), to be followed thereafter by 'the sons of Abraham' (1.28), including 'the sons of Keturah, Abraham's concubine' (1.32). The Annalists do not explain why this significant character has a dual designation or what the names might mean, but Genesis partly does so when it has Yahweh appear to Abram and say to him, 'This is my covenant with you: You shall be the father of a multitude of nations. No longer shall your name be "Abram" [i.e. "exalted father"], but your name shall be "Abraham" [i.e. "father of a multitude"], for I have made you the father of a multitude of nations' (Genesis 17.4-5). Genesis closes the chapter on his life as follows: 'This is the length of Abraham's life, 175 years. Abraham breathed his last and died in a good old age, an old man and full of years, and was gathered to his people. His sons Isaac and Ishmael buried him in the cave of Machpelah... There Abraham was buried, with his wife Sarah' (Genesis 25.7-10). The Annals do not relate any of that, but they do make a number of references to this great patriarch, such as in the psalm of thanksgiving sung on the day that David brought the sacred ark into the city of Jerusalem ('Remember his covenant forever, the word that he commanded for a thousand generations, the covenant that he made with Abraham, his sworn promise to Isaac, which he confirmed to Jacob as a statute, to Israel as an everlasting covenant, saying, "To you I will give the land of Canaan as your portion for an inheritance"' [1 Chron. 16.15-18]) and in the prayer of Jehoshaphat on the day he prepared for battle against a great multitude ('Did you not, O our god, drive out the inhabitants of this land before your people Israel, and give it forever to the descendants of your friend Abraham?' [2 Chron. 20.7]).

- **Isaac**

  The patriarch who links Abraham to Israel (1.28, 34). His name 'he laughs' is explained in Genesis 21.1-6.

- **Ishmael**

  Patriarch of the Ishmaelite peoples catalogued in 1.29-31. His name 'El [the deity] hears' is explained in Genesis 16.11.

- **Zimran**

  Patriarch of the Zimranites (not further itemized). The Annals list his mother's name (1.32) but not Isaac's mother's name!

- **Jokshan**

  Patriarch of the two branches of Jokshanites (the tribes of Sheba and Dedan) listed in 1.32.

- **Medan**

  Patriarch of the Medanites (not further itemized—and since the name means 'strife', they are perhaps best left alone).

- **Midian**

  Patriarch of the five branches of Midianites (the tribes of Ephah, Epher, Hanoch, Abida and Eldaah) listed in 1.33.

- **Ishbak**

  Patriarch of the Ishbakites (not further itemized—thus his name 'he [i.e. the deity] lets [him] go' seems symbolic).

- **Shuah**

  Patriarch of the Shuahites (not further itemized—thus his name 'he melts away' or 'he vanishes' seems very apt).

- ● **Esau**

  Isaac's firstborn is superseded by his younger brother Israel, even though Esau's descendants technically had a head start and were able to get their act together more quickly, to judge by the list of 'kings who reigned in the land of Edom [i.e. Esau's land] before any king reigned over the Israelites' (1.43). The Esauites (Edomites) are at first catalogued under five sub-groups (1.35) plus an additional group (1.38), and then divided into eleven clans (1.51-54). The names 'Edom' and 'Esau' ('red' and 'hairy') are explained in Genesis 25.5.

- ● **Israel**

  The twenty-second man to occupy the line of destiny is the eponymous ancestor of the Israelites. He is alternatively known as 'Jacob'—as in the hymnic parallelism employed in 16.13: 'O offspring of his servant Israel, children of Jacob, his chosen ones'—though the Annalists do not pause to relate the Israelite legend of how this people came to be called something other than Jacobites. For such matters, Genesis 25.26 (on the name 'Jacob') and 32.28 (on the name 'Israel') may be consulted.

- **Reuben**

  Patriarch of the Reubenites catalogued in 5.1-10. His name 'behold a son' is vaguely explained in Genesis 29.32.

- **Simeon**

  Patriarch of the Simeonites catalogued in 4.24-43. His name 'hearing' or 'listening' is explained in Genesis 29.33.

- **Levi**

  Patriarch of the Levites catalogued in 6.1-81. His name 'the one who joins' is explained in Genesis 29.34.

- **Judah**

  Patriarch of the Judahites catalogued in 2.3– 4.23. His name 'praise' is explained in Genesis 29.35.

- **Issachar**

  Patriarch of the Issacharites catalogued in 7.1-5. His name 'he [i.e. the deity] recompenses' is explained in Genesis 30.18.

- **Zebulun**

  Patriarch of the Zebulunites (not catalogued). His name 'honour' is explained in Genesis 30.20.

- **Dan**

  Patriarch of the Danites (not catalogued). His name 'he [i.e. the deity] has judged' is explained in Genesis 30.6.

- **Joseph**

  Patriarch of the tribes catalogued in 5.23-26 and 7.14-29. His name 'he [i.e. the deity] adds' is explained in Genesis 30.24.

- **Benjamin**

  Patriarch of the Benjaminites catalogued in 7.6-12 and 8.1-40. His name 'right-hand son' is recounted in Genesis 35.18.

- **Naphtali**

  Patriarch of the Naphtalites briefly outlined in 7.13. His name 'I have wrestled' is explained in Genesis 30.8.

- **Gad**

  Patriarch of the Gadites catalogued in 5.11-22. His name 'good fortune' is explained in Genesis 30.11.

- **Asher**

  Patriarch of the Asherites catalogued in 7.30-40. His name 'happiness' is explained in Genesis 30.13.

- **Er**

  Judah's firstborn is said to be a very wicked man (2.3). The very same assessment is made of him in Genesis 38.7.

- **Onan**

  The next son is not assessed in the Annals (though he is—rather salaciously—in Genesis 38.8-10).

- **Shelah**

  The last of Judah's 'Canaanite' sons (2.3), the subject of some information in Genesis 38.11-26 and Numbers 26.20.

- **Perez**

  The twenty-fourth man to occupy the line of destiny (2.4). His name 'breach' is explained in Genesis 38.29.

- **Zerah**

  Patriarch of the five branches of Zerahites listed in 2.6. His name 'brightness' is explained in Genesis 38.30.

- **Hezron**

  The twenty-fifth man to occupy the line of destiny is the eponymous ancestor of 'the clan of the Hezronites' (as they are designated in Numbers 26.21). The Annalists furnish us with some vignettes from the legends concerning Hezron, telling us that he 'went in to the daughter of Machir father of Gilead, whom he married when he was 60 years old, and she bore him Segub' (2.21), and further that 'after the death of Hezron, in Caleb-ephrathah, Abijah wife of Hezron bore him Ashhur, father of Tekoa' (2.24); they also speak of various towns and villages inhabited by certain groups of Hezronites, including the towns of Havvoth-jair and Kenath (2.22-23), but they make no mention of a settlement called Hezron (which is listed as part of 'the lot for the tribe of the people of Judah according to their families' in Joshua 15.1-3). The name 'Hezron' in fact has to do with 'settlement' or 'enclosure', and thus may designate a more settled, less nomadic clan.

- **Hamul**

  The other division of Perezites are those that belong to 'the clan of the Hamulites' (as they are designated in Numbers 26.21). Nothing is said of this clan in the Annals, and nor are any stories told about their eponymous ancestor, even though his name—which means 'the one who is spared' or 'he for whom compassion is felt' (it is in the form of the passive participle of the Hebrew verb *chamal*)—cries out for a supporting legend in the style of those concerning Peleg ('the name of the one was Peleg, for in his days the earth was divided', 1.17), Jabez ('and his mother named him Jabez, saying, "Because I bore him in pain"', 4.9), or Beriah ('and he named him Beriah, because disaster had befallen his house', 7.23). The verb *chamal* is used in 2 Chron. 36.15 ('because he had compassion on his people'), but the naming of Hamul is not explained.

- **Jerahmeel**

  Hezron's firstborn is superseded by his younger brother Ram, but apparently bears him no grudge since he bestows the name of Ram ('exalted one') upon his own firstborn son (2.25). As for his own name, 'Jerahmeel' means 'El [the deity] has compassion'.

- **Ram**

  The twenty-sixth man to occupy the line of destiny does not appear to produce as extended a family as his brothers, but only one offspring is needed from him for the line to continue (2.9-10). His name of 'exalted one' is reminiscent of his ancestor Abram ('exalted father'), a.k.a. 'Abraham'.

- **Chelubai/Caleb**

  The Annalists introduce some confusion at this point by listing 'Chelubai' (2.9) but then taking up the genealogy with 'Caleb son of Hezron' and 'brother of Jerahmeel' (2.18, 42). Both forms of the name (*kluvay* and *kalev* in Hebrew) seem related to the word 'dog' (*kelev*).

- **Segub**

  Having originally listed just three sons of Hezron (2.9), the Annals append a short tale of how the man had another son following a new marriage at a more advanced age (2.21: 'Hezron went in to the daughter of Machir...whom he married when he was 60 years old, and she bore him Segub').

- **Ashhur**

  Despite the earlier suggestion of just three sons (2.9), a further episode is related concerning yet another, this one being born posthumously (2.24: 'after the death of Hezron, in Caleb-ephrathah, Abijah wife of Hezron bore him Ashhur, father of Tekoa').

● **Amminadab**

The twenty-seventh generation sees the figure of Amminadab standing on the line of destiny (2.10). It is noticeable at this point, as mentioned in the introductory comments to this parade of the generations, that as we move now through the tribe of Judah towards the decisive juncture of King David, the figures parading before us are lingering somewhat longer than did the earlier characters. Before, when there had been a number of generations to move through without other lines branching off, the Annalists had contented themselves with simply listing the names one after the other—such as 'Adam, Seth, Enosh' etc. in 1.1-3 or 'Shem, Arpachshad, Shelah' etc. in 1.24-27—but now the formulation has become more elongated: 'Ram became the father of Amminadab, and Amminadab became the father of Nahshon, prince of the sons of Judah; and Nahshon became the father of Salma, and Salma became the father of Boaz, and Boaz became the father of Obed, and Obed became the father of Jesse' (2.10-12). As for Amminadab himself, whose name means 'my kinsman is noble', it seems that becoming 'the father of Nahshon, prince of the sons of Judah' is his main claim to fame in the Hebrew traditions, to judge by the common reference in the book of Numbers to 'Nahshon son of Amminadab' (e.g. Numbers 1.7; 2.3). But his second claim to fame is being the father of a daughter who is not mentioned in the Annalists' lists (despite their interest in matters concerning the Aaronites and other clans within the tribe of Levi), but is referred to in Exodus 6.23: 'Aaron married Elisheba, daughter of Amminadab and sister of Nahshon, and she bore him Nadab, Abihu, Eleazar, and Ithamar'. Such a marriage linking the royal line of David with the priestly line of Aaron might be seen as something very significant indeed, but the Annalists pay it no attention.

● Nahshon

The twenty-eighth generation sees the figure of Nahshon standing on the line of destiny (2.10). The Annalists do him the honour of styling him as 'Nahshon, prince of the sons of Judah', but say no more about him. The compilers of the book of Numbers have rather more to say, putting him and his tribe in first place in the order of encampment and marching for the Israelites: 'The Israelites shall camp each in their respective regiments, under ensigns by their ancestral houses; they shall camp facing the tent of meeting on every side. Those to camp on the east side toward the sunrise shall be of the regimental encampment of Judah by companies, and the leader of the people of Judah shall be Nahshon son of Amminadab, with a company as enrolled of 74,600... They shall set out first on the march' (Numbers 2.2-4). So it is that 'the standard of the camp of Judah set out first, company by company, and over the whole company was Nahshon son of Amminadab' (Numbers 10.14). The same man is in the front position when it comes to the Israelite leaders presenting offerings for the dedication of the altar: 'The one who presented his offering the first day was Nahshon son of Amminadab, of the tribe of Judah; his offering was one silver plate weighing 130 shekels, one silver basin weighing 70 shekels, according to the shekel of the sanctuary, both of them full of choice flour mixed with oil for a grain offering; one golden dish weighing ten shekels, full of incense; one young bull, one ram, one male lamb a year old for a burnt offering; one male goat for a sin offering; and for the sacrifice of well-being, two oxen, five rams, five male goats, and five male lambs a year old. This was the offering of Nahshon son of Amminadab' (Numbers 7.12-17).

• Salma

The twenty-ninth generation sees the figure of Salma standing on the line of destiny within the sequence 'Nahshon became the father of Salma, and Salma became the father of Boaz' (2.11). A little later on the Annalists also cite a 'Salma father of Bethlehem' (2.51) and go on to list 'the sons of Salma: Bethlehem, the Netophathites, Atroth-beth-joab, and half of the Manahathites, the Zorites' (2.54), but all of those communities are located within the Calebite ambit (2.42-55). The possibility of confusion among the genealogists is evident, given the somewhat shambolic nature of the Calebite genealogy in the Annals and at the same time given that the scroll of Ruth (at Ruth 1.22– 2.1) locates Boaz (the son of Salma according to 1 Chron. 2.11) as a Bethlehemite (the offspring of Salma according to 1 Chron. 2.51, 54). For that matter, the Ruth scroll evidences two different though closely related names for the character in focus here, while agreeing fully with the Annalists on the other names in the sequence. Ruth 4.18-22 reads: 'Now these are the descendants of Perez: Perez became the father of Hezron, Hezron of Ram, Ram of Amminadab, Amminadab of Nahshon, Nahshon of Salmah [representing a slightly different spelling to that of 'Salma' in the Annals], Salmon [putting forward immediately a different ending to that of the 'Salmah' the scroll had just used] of Boaz, Boaz of Obed, Obed of Jesse, and Jesse of David'. Evidently the Annalists were not the only ones to find Salma a somewhat slippery character. But perhaps the last word on him may be taken from a much later document, the Gospel of Matthew, which claims that 'Salmon was the father of Boaz by Rahab' (Matthew 1.5), thus connecting this character with the famous prostitute of Jericho (Joshua 2.1-21; 4.22-25).

● Boaz

The thirtieth generation sees the figure of Boaz standing on the line of destiny (2.12). A delightful tale about how he comes to be the father of Obed and thus the great-grand-father of David is told in the scroll of Ruth, in which Boaz, 'a prominent rich man' (Ruth 2.1), and 'Ruth the Moabitess' (v. 2) meet and eventually marry. The first conversation between the hero—whose name fittingly has to do with 'strength'—and the heroine—whose name may have something to do with 'companionship'—runs as follows: 'Boaz said to Ruth, "Listen, my daughter, do not go to glean in another field or leave this one, but keep close to my young women. Keep your eyes on the field that is being reaped, and follow behind them. I have ordered the young men not to bother you. If you get thirsty, go to the vessels and drink from what the young men have drawn." Then she fell prostrate, with her face to the ground, and said to him, "Why have I found favour in your sight, that you should take notice of me, when I am a foreigner?" But Boaz answered her, "All that you have done for your mother-in-law since the death of your husband has been fully told me, and how you left your father and mother and your native land and came to a people that you did not know before. May Yahweh reward you for your deeds, and may you have a full reward from Yahweh, the god of Israel, under whose wings you have come for refuge!" Then she said, "May I continue to find favour in your sight, my lord, for you have comforted me and spoken kindly to your servant, even though I am not one of your servants"' (Ruth 2.8-12). From this first encounter matters develop apace and, after certain complications are resolved, 'Boaz took Ruth and she became his wife; when they came together, Yahweh made her conceive, and she bore a son' (Ruth 4.3). The line of destiny continues.

• Obed

The thirty-first generation sees the figure of Obed standing on the line of destiny (2.12). Again, as in the case of his father Boaz, one can turn to the scroll of Ruth to see a tale in which he plays a part, for in that story it is the birth of Obed which brings happiness to his mother Ruth and her mother-in-law Naomi, both of whom had been widowed, childless, and vulnerable early in the tale. The story culminates in the following narrative: 'Then Boaz said to the elders and all the people, "Today you are witnesses that I have acquired from the hand of Naomi…Ruth the Moabite, the widow of Mahlon, to be my wife…" Then all the people who were at the gate, along with the elders, said, "We are witnesses. May Yahweh make the woman who is coming into your house like Rachel and Leah, who together built up the house of Israel. May you produce children in Ephrathah and bestow a name in Bethlehem; and, through the children that Yahweh will give you by this young woman, may your house be like the house of Perez, whom Tamar bore to Judah." So Boaz took Ruth and she became his wife. When they came together, Yahweh made her conceive, and she bore a son. Then the women said to Naomi, "Blessed be Yahweh, who has not left you this day without next-of-kin; and may his name be renowned in Israel! He shall be to you a restorer of life and a nourisher of your old age; for your daughter-in-law who loves you, who is more to you than seven sons, has borne him." Then Naomi took the child and laid him in her bosom, and became his nurse. The women of the neighbourhood gave him a name, saying, "A son has been born to Naomi". They named him Obed; he became the father of Jesse, the father of David' (Ruth 4.9-17). Quite why they give him the name 'servant' is not clear, but they may be thinking of it as the short form of 'Obadiah' ('servant of Yah[weh]').

• Jesse

The thirty-second generation sees the figure of Jesse standing on the line of destiny (2.12) and on the cusp of the new era that will begin through the agency of his youngest son David. As the father of the founding monarch, his name has an honoured place in the Annalists' scheme of things, although he plays no active role in the stories they tell of how Yahweh 'turned the kingdom over to David son of Jesse' (10.14) and how the Israelites came to proclaim, 'We are yours, O David; and with you, O son of Jesse!' (12.18). King David will take pride in the notion that Yahweh 'chose Judah as leader, and in the house of Judah my father's house' (28.4), but it is not clear whether this implies that Jesse had princely status in his own time, as his ancestor Nahshon had had in his time (2.10); it may be that we are rather to suppose that the divine choice of the house of Jesse was only recognized when 'David son of Jesse reigned over all Israel' (29.26). Yet King David is also represented as praying at one point, 'Let your hand, O Yahweh my god, be against me and against my father's house, but do not let your people be plagued!' (21.17); it is a noble rhetorical gesture, this willingness to sacrifice all that he has achieved for himself and his family if only the divine wrath will pass from his nation, but in the story-world of the Annalists the house of Jesse is secure, and will survive even the great wrath of Yahweh that he will manifest in the Babylonian destruction of Jerusalem and deportation of the descendant of Jesse reigning at the time (2 Chron. 36.15-21). And beyond these Annals too, in certain prophetic traditions of ancient Israel, the name of Jesse will still resonate: 'A shoot shall come out from the stump of Jesse, and a branch shall grow out of his roots' (Isaiah 11.1).

- **David's brothers**

  Lining up before what turns out to be the central character of David are no less than six individuals who will need to stand aside and allow the procession of generations to become a Davidic affair from this point onwards. These older sons of Jesse are named as 'Eliab his firstborn, Abinadab the second, Shimea the third, Nethanel the fourth, Raddai the fifth, [and] Ozem the sixth' (2.13-15). But Yahweh will pass over them all to 'take delight in making [David] king over all Israel' (28.4), even though he is merely 'David the seventh [son]' (2.15).

- **David**

  The thirty-third man to occupy the line of destiny is the unparalleled David. At first sight he does not seem particularly special (even with his name meaning 'the beloved one'), since he comes in at Number Seven in the seven sons of Jesse (2.15), but the line of descent from him will carry all before it in 3.1-24 while his older brothers' families lie uncharted—and once the genealogical material is completed, it will be tales of David (in 1 Chron. 10.14– 29.30) and his successors (in 2 Chron. 1.1– 36.21) that will fill much of the Annals.

- **David's sisters**

  Also listed alongside the special man David in this procession that for the most part is comprised of men, are two sisters, Zeruiah and Abigail (2.16). The three sons of Zeruiah—namely Abishai, Joab, and Asahel (2.16)—and the one son of Abigail—namely 'Amasa, whose father was Jether the Ishmaelite' (1.17)—are also cited. Two of these nephews of David appear in his story: Abishai and Joab both take leading roles among his fighting men (e.g. 11.6, 20; 19.10-15), the latter taking the key post of army commander (18.15; 27.34).

• Solomon's older brothers

Like his father before him, Solomon is well down the list of sons, behind 'the firstborn Amnon', 'the second Daniel', 'the third Absalom', 'the fourth Adonijah', 'the fifth Shephatiah', and 'the sixth Ithream'—all half-brothers of Solomon and all born in Hebron (3.1-3)—as well as three full brothers (namely 'Shimea, Shobab, [and] Nathan') apparently born in Jerusalem before Solomon comes onto the scene (2.5—note the expression 'four by Bath-shua, daughter of Ammiel'). But Yahweh will pass over them all to choose Solomon (28.5).

• Solomon

The thirty-fourth man to occupy the line of destiny appears in the list of royal sons at the central position, with nine brothers older and nine younger than the one who will inherit the legacy of David. The names of his brothers listed on either side of him at this point will never be uttered again, but his highly redolent name—'for his name shall be Solomon (*shlomo*) and I will give peace (*shalom*) and quiet to Israel in his days' (22.9)—will resonate continually in the Annals (particularly in 1 Chronicles 22– 2 Chronicles 9).

• Solomon's younger brothers

Nine further sons are listed as having been born to David in Jerusalem, namely Ibhar, Elishama, Eliphelet, Nogah, Nepheg, Japhia, Elishama, Eliada, and Eliphelet (3.6-8), and this does not include an unspecified number of 'sons of the concubines' (3.9). There are some difficulties with the list, in that the names 'Elishama' and 'Eliphelet' appear here twice; later in the tale (at 14.5, where David's Jerusalemite sons are listed again), 'Elishua' and 'Elpelet' substitute for one pair of these brothers, while 'Eliada' turns into 'Beeliada'.

• Tamar

As in the previous generation, where in fact two sisters of David were mentioned, the Annalists bring themselves to include a female name among the largely male character procession. However, they cannot bring themselves to say anything about her, even though the poets of Israel might rhapsodize over her name (as in Psalm 92.12—'the righteous flourish like Tamar [a palm tree], and grow like Erez [a cedar tree] in Lebanon'—and in Song of Songs 7.7: 'How fair and pleasant you are, O loved one… You are stately as a Tamar').

● **Rehoboam**

The thirty-fifth generation witnesses the reign of Rehoboam.
He is listed in the Davidic genealogy in 1 Chron. 3.10, and an
account of his reign is presented in 2 Chron. 10.1– 12.16,
where we see the great irony of this name 'Rehoboam' (meaning 'increase of the nation') being borne by the man under
whose stewardship ten of the twelve tribes of Israel are lost
to the kingdom: 'When all Israel saw that the king would not
listen to them, the people answered the king, "What share do
we have in David? We have no inheritance in the son of Jesse.
Each of you to your tents, O Israel! Look now to your own
house, O David!" So all Israel departed to their tents, and
Rehoboam reigned [only] over the people of Israel who were
living in the cities of Judah [and Benjamin]… So Israel has
been in rebellion against the house of David to this day'
(2 Chron. 10.16-19). Some further information of a genealogical kind is supplied by the Annalists later in the story:
'Rehoboam took as his wife Mahalath daughter of Jerimoth
son of David, and of Abihail daughter of Eliab son of Jesse.
She bore him sons: Jeush, Shemariah, and Zaham. After her
he took Maacah daughter of Absalom, who bore him Abijah,
Attai, Ziza, and Shelomith. Rehoboam loved Maacah daughter
of Absalom more than all his other wives and concubines (he
took 18 wives and 60 concubines, and became the father of
28 sons and 60 daughters)' (2 Chron. 11.18-23). The final
summation of his reign in the Annals reads as follows: 'Rehoboam was 41 years old when he began to reign, and he
reigned for 17 years in Jerusalem, the city that Yahweh had
chosen out of all the tribes of Israel to put his name there.
His mother's name was Naamah the Ammonite. He did evil,
for he did not set his heart to seek Yahweh… He slept with
his ancestors and was buried in the city of David. His son
Abijah succeeded him' (2 Chron. 12.13-14, 16).

● Abijah

The thirty-sixth generation witnesses the reign of Abijah. He is listed in the Davidic genealogy in 1 Chron. 3.10, and an account of his reign is presented in 2 Chron. 13.1-22. That account opens with the following information: 'In the eighteenth year of King Jeroboam [of the breakaway kingdom of Israel], Abijah began to reign over Judah. He reigned for three years in Jerusalem. His mother's name was Micaiah daughter of Uriel of Gibeah' (2 Chron. 13.1-2). The major incident of his reign is a decisive battle between the northern Israelite forces and his own Judahite troops, and before the battle the Annalists have him give a rousing speech which ends with the call, 'O Israelites, do not fight against Yahweh, the god of your fathers!' (2 Chron. 13.12), exactly the kind of saying that ought to be attributed to a man whose name means 'Yah [i.e. Yahweh] is my father'. The Annalists then relate that Yahweh 'defeated Jeroboam and all Israel before Abijah and Judah. The Israelites fled before Judah, and the deity gave them into their hands. Abijah and his army defeated them with a great slaughter; 500,000 picked men of Israel fell slain. Thus the Israelites were subdued at that time, and the people of Judah prevailed, because they relied on Yahweh, the god of their fathers' (2 Chron. 13.15-18). The Annalists are pleased to relate a difference in fate between the northern and southern rulers: 'Jeroboam did not recover his power in the days of Abijah; Yahweh struck him down, and he died. But Abijah grew strong. He took 14 wives, and became the father of 22 sons and 16 daughters. The rest of the acts of Abijah, his behaviour and his deeds, are written in the story of the prophet Iddo. So Abijah slept with his ancestors, and they buried him in the city of David. His son Asa succeeded him' (2 Chron. 13.20– 14.1).

• Asa

The thirty-seventh generation witnesses the reign of Asa. He is listed in the Davidic genealogy in 1 Chron. 3.10, and an account of his reign is presented in 2 Chron. 14.1– 16.14. That account begins by stating that 'in his days the land had rest for ten years. Asa did what was good and right in the sight of his god Yahweh. He took away the foreign altars and the high places, broke down the pillars, hewed down the sacred poles, and commanded Judah to seek Yahweh, the god of their fathers, and to keep the law and the commandment. He also removed from all the cities of Judah the high places and the incense altars. And the kingdom had rest under him. He built fortified cities in Judah while the land had rest. He had no war in those years, for Yahweh gave him peace' (2 Chron. 14.1-6). Moreover, 'King Asa even removed his mother Maacah from being queen mother because she had made an abominable image for Asherah... The heart of Asa was true all his days' (2 Chron. 15.16-17). However, 'in the thirty-ninth year of his reign Asa was diseased in his feet, and his disease became severe; yet even in his disease he did not seek Yahweh, but sought help from physicians' (2 Chron. 16.12). The writers do not spell out that the name 'Asa' is a term for 'healer' or 'physician' in the Aramaic language (a language closely related to Hebrew and the *lingua franca* of the surrounding world in those days), but the irony of a physician who cannot heal himself is not necessarily lost on the audience. Thus it is that 'Asa slept with his ancestors, dying in the forty-first year of his reign. They buried him in the tomb that he had hewn out for himself in the city of David. They laid him on a bier that had been filled with various kinds of spices prepared by the perfumer's art, and they made a very great fire in his honour. His son Jehoshaphat succeeded him' (2 Chron. 16.13– 17.1).

• Jehoshaphat

The thirty-eighth generation witnesses the reign of Jehoshaphat. He is listed in the Davidic genealogy in 1 Chron. 3.10, and an account of his reign is presented in 2 Chron. 17.1– 20.37. Essentially, according to that account, 'the realm of Jehoshaphat was quiet, for his god gave him rest all around. So Jehoshaphat reigned over Judah. He was 35 years old when he began to reign, and he reigned for 25 years in Jerusalem. His mother's name was Azubah daughter of Shilhi. He walked in the way of his father Asa and did not turn aside from it, doing what was right in the sight of Yahweh' (2 Chron. 20.30-32). His name 'Jehoshaphat', which carries the meaning 'Yah[weh] has judged', is reflected in one of this king's claims to fame, in that 'he appointed judges in the land in all the fortified cities of Judah, and said to the judges, "Consider what you are doing, for you judge not on behalf of human beings but on Yahweh's behalf; he is with you in giving judgment. Now, let the fear of Yahweh be upon you; take care what you do, for there is no perversion of justice with our god Yahweh, or partiality, or taking of bribes"' (2 Chron. 19.5-7). However, despite his good sense with that policy initiative, some time later 'King Jehoshaphat of Judah joined with King Ahaziah of Israel, who did wickedly. He joined him in building ships to go to Tarshish; they built the ships in Ezion-geber. Then Eliezer son of Dodavahu of Mareshah prophesied against Jehoshaphat, saying, "Because you have joined with Ahaziah, Yahweh will destroy what you have made". And the ships were wrecked and were not able to go to Tarshish. Jehoshaphat slept with his ancestors and was buried with his ancestors in the city of David. His son Jehoram succeeded him' (2 Chron. 20.35– 21.1).

• Joram

The thirty-ninth generation witnesses the reign of Joram. He is listed in the Davidic genealogy as 'Joram' in 1 Chron. 3.11, and an account of his reign under the longer form of his name as 'Jehoram' is presented in 2 Chron. 21.1-20. The variation in name does not change its meaning, which is 'Yah [i.e. Yahweh] is exalted', but the man does not match the sentiment, for we are told that 'when Jehoram had ascended the throne of his father and was established, he put all his brothers to the sword, and also some of the officials of Israel. Jehoram was 32 years old when he began to reign, and he reigned for eight years in Jerusalem. He walked in the way of the kings of Israel, as the house of Ahab had done; for the daughter of Ahab was his wife. He did what was evil in the sight of Yahweh. Yet Yahweh would not destroy the house of David because of the covenant that he had made with David, and since he had promised to give a lamp to him and to his descendants forever' (2 Chron. 21.4-7). Nonetheless, 'Yahweh struck him in his bowels with an incurable disease. In the course of time, at the end of two years, his bowels came out because of the disease, and he died in great agony. His people made no fire in his honour, like the fires made for his ancestors... He departed with no one's regret. They buried him in the city of David, but not in the tombs of the kings' (2 Chron. 21.18-20). The Annalists also supply some extra genealogical details when they tell J[eh]oram's story, namely that he 'had brothers, the sons of Jehoshaphat: Azariah, Jehiel, Zechariah, Azariah, Michael, and Shephatiah; all these were the sons of King Jehoshaphat of Judah. Their father gave them many gifts, of silver, gold, and valuable possessions, together with fortified cities in Judah; but he gave the kingdom to Jehoram, because he was the firstborn' (2 Chron. 21.2-3).

● Ahaziah

The fortieth generation witnesses the reign of Ahaziah. He is
listed in the Davidic genealogy in 1 Chron. 3.11, and an
account of his reign is presented in 2 Chron. 22.1-9. That account begins as follows: 'The inhabitants of Jerusalem made
Jehoram's youngest son Ahaziah king as his successor; for the
troops who came with the Arabs to the camp had killed all
the older sons. So Ahaziah son of Jehoram reigned as king of
Judah. Ahaziah was 42 years old when he began to reign, and
he reigned for one year in Jerusalem. His mother's name was
Athaliah, a granddaughter of Omri. He also walked in the
ways of the house of Ahab, for his mother was his counsellor
in doing wickedly. He did what was evil in the sight of
Yahweh, as the house of Ahab had done; for after the death of
his father they were his counsellors, to his ruin' (2 Chron.
22.1-4). He certainly does come to a ruinous end, and indeed
his name 'Ahaziah'—which means 'Yah [i.e. Yahweh] has
seized'—symbolizes his fate, for 'it was divinely ordained that
the downfall of Ahaziah should come about through his going
to visit [King Jehoram of Israel, son of King Ahab]. For when
he came there he went out with Jehoram to meet Jehu son
of Nimshi, whom Yahweh had anointed to destroy the house
of Ahab. When Jehu was executing judgment on the house of
Ahab, he met the officials of Judah and the sons of Ahaziah's
brothers, who attended Ahaziah, and he killed them. He
searched for Ahaziah, who was captured while hiding in Samaria and was brought to Jehu, and put to death. They buried
him, for they said, "He is the grandson of Jehoshaphat, who
sought Yahweh with all his heart". And the house of Ahaziah
had no one able to rule the kingdom' (2 Chron. 22.7-9).

• Joash

The forty-first generation witnesses the reign of Joash. He is listed in the Davidic genealogy in 1 Chron. 3.11, and an account of his reign is presented in 2 Chron. 24.1-27 (after a preamble recounting a non-Davidic interregnum in 2 Chron. 22.10– 23.31). The Annalists report that 'Joash was seven years old when he began to reign, and he reigned for 40 years in Jerusalem. His mother's name was Zibiah of Beersheba. Joash did what was right in the sight of Yahweh all the days of the priest Jehoiada. Jehoiada got two wives for him, and he became the father of sons and daughters' (2 Chron. 24.1-3). But after the death of his mentor Jehoiada, Joash became a less honourable king, and eventually he suffers a catastrophic defeat at the hands of 'the army of Aram'; this is Yahweh's doing, say the Annalists, 'because [the people of Judah] had abandoned Yahweh, the god of their fathers. Thus [the army of Aram] executed judgment on Joash. When they had withdrawn, leaving him severely wounded, his servants conspired against him because of the blood of the son of the priest Jehoiada, and they killed him on his bed. So he died; and they buried him in the city of David, but they did not bury him in the tombs of the kings' (2 Chron. 24.24-25). The story may be developing a certain ironic spin on the king's name 'Joash', for it appears to mean 'he [i.e. the deity] has healed', whereas in fact the deity does not heal him after he is left severely wounded by the foreign forces, on account of his not having listened to the divine word that had been preached to him by the son of his former mentor. The parallels with his descendant Josiah, whose name combines the same verbal element as that in Joash but makes explicit the name of the deity (i.e. 'Yah[weh] has healed') and whose fate is remarkably similar, are too marked to be entirely coincidental in the Annalists' story-world.

● **Amaziah**

The forty-second generation witnesses the reign of Amaziah. He is listed in the Davidic genealogy in 1 Chron. 3.12, and an account of his reign is presented in 2 Chron. 25.1-28. That account begins as follows: 'Amaziah was 25 years old when he began to reign, and he reigned for 29 years in Jerusalem. His mother's name was Jehoaddan of Jerusalem. He did what was right in the sight of Yahweh, yet not with a true heart' (2 Chron. 25.1-2). Indeed later in his reign Amaziah compromises himself, in that 'he brought the gods of the people of Seir, set them up as his gods, and worshipped them, making offerings to them. Yahweh was angry with Amaziah and sent to him a prophet, who said to him, "Why have you resorted to a people's gods who could not deliver their own people from your hand?"' (2 Chron. 25.14-15)—in other words, the king had forgotten his own name, for 'Amaziah' means 'Yah [i.e. Yahweh] is powerful'. The lesson that the god of Israel is indeed the powerful one while the gods of Seir are powerless is taught to King Amaziah through Yahweh determining 'to hand them [i.e. Judah] over [to Israel], because they had sought the gods of Edom. Thus King Joash of Israel went up; he and King Amaziah of Judah faced one another in battle at Beth-shemesh, which belongs to Judah, and Judah was defeated by Israel' (2 Chron. 25.20). And for good measure, 'from the time that Amaziah turned away from Yahweh they made a conspiracy against him in Jerusalem, and he fled to Lachish. But they sent after him to Lachish, and killed him there. They brought him back on horses; he was buried with his ancestors in the city of David. Then all the people of Judah took Uzziah, who was 16 years old, and made him king to succeed his father Amaziah' (2 Chron. 25.23– 26.1).

● **Azariah**

The forty-third generation witnesses the reign of Azariah. He is listed in the Davidic genealogy as 'Azariah' in 1 Chron. 3.12, and an account of his reign under the somewhat different name of 'Uzziah' is presented in 2 Chron. 26.1-23. The change of names is not explained, but we are probably meant to think of this individual as having adopted a new name upon his accession to the throne, and indeed the throne-name 'Uzziah' (i.e. 'Yah[weh] is strong') has more metaphorical force in the story of his reign than does the childhood-name 'Azariah' (i.e. 'Yah[weh] has helped'), for we read of the king's ill-advised attempt to perform a priestly act in the temple of Yahweh, with disastrous consequences: 'When the chief priest Azariah [not to be confused with the king formerly known as Azariah but now known as Uzziah] and all the priests looked at him, he was leprous in his forehead. They hurried him out [of the temple], and he himself hurried to get out, because Yahweh had struck him. King Uzziah was leprous to the day of his death, and being leprous lived in a separate house, for he was excluded from the house of Yahweh. His son Jotham was in charge of the palace of the king, governing the people of the land… Uzziah slept with his ancestors; they buried him near his ancestors in the burial field that belonged to the kings, for they said, "He is leprous". His son Jotham succeeded him' (2 Chron. 26.20-23). In summary, 'Uzziah was 16 years old when he began to reign, and he reigned for 52 years in Jerusalem. His mother's name was Jecoliah of Jerusalem… He had set himself to seek the deity in the days of Zechariah, who instructed him in the fear of the divine; and as long as he sought Yahweh, the deity made him prosper… But when he had become strong he grew proud, to his destruction, for he became false to his god Yahweh' (2 Chron. 26.3, 5, 16).

● Jotham

The forty-fourth generation witnesses the reign of Jotham. He is listed in the Davidic genealogy in 1 Chron. 3.12, and an account of his reign is presented in 2 Chron. 27.1-9: 'Jotham was 25 years old when he began to reign, and he reigned for 16 years in Jerusalem. His mother's name was Jerushah daughter of Zadok. He did what was right in the sight of Yahweh just as his father Uzziah had done—only he did not invade the temple of Yahweh. But the people still followed corrupt practices. He built the upper gate of the house of Yahweh, and did extensive building on the wall of Ophel. Moreover he built cities in the hill country of Judah, and forts and towers on the wooded hills. He fought with the king of the Ammonites and prevailed against them. The Ammonites gave him that year 100 talents of silver, 10,000 cors of wheat, and 10,000 cors of barley. The Ammonites paid him the same amount in the second and the third years. So Jotham became strong because he ordered his ways before his god Yahweh. Now the rest of the acts of Jotham, and all his wars and his ways, are written in the Book of the Kings of Israel and Judah. He was 25 years old when he began to reign, and he reigned for 16 years in Jerusalem. Jotham slept with his ancestors, and they buried him in the city of David; and his son Ahaz succeeded him.' That is in fact the complete tale of Jotham in these Annals, with twice-told statistics at the beginning and the end of the account in regard to his age at his coronation and the length of his reign, and in between a tale which, though briefly told, befits a monarch whose name means 'Yah[weh] is perfect'. Such a one 'did what was right in the sight of Yahweh' (v. 2) and 'became strong because he ordered his ways before his god Yahweh' (v. 6); the Annalists evidently believe that not much more needs to be said.

• Ahaz

The forty-fifth generation witnesses the reign of Ahaz. He is listed in the Davidic genealogy in 1 Chron. 3.13, and an account of his reign is presented in 2 Chron. 28.1-27. That account begins as follows: 'Ahaz was 20 years old when he began to reign, and he reigned for 16 years in Jerusalem. He did not do what was right in the sight of Yahweh, as his ancestor David had done, but he walked in the ways of the kings of Israel. He even made cast images for the Baals; and he made offerings in the valley of the son of Hinnom, and made his sons pass through fire, according to the abominable practices of the nations whom Yahweh drove out before the people of Israel. He sacrificed and made offerings on the high places, on the hills, and under every green tree. Therefore his god Yahweh gave him into the hand of the king of Aram, who defeated him and took captive a great number of his people and brought them to Damascus. He was also given into the hand of the king of Israel, who defeated him with great slaughter' (2 Chron. 28.1-5). All of this is appropriate for a king named 'Ahaz', which means 'he [i.e. the deity] has seized' (one might compare the similar destinies of his ancestor Ahaziah and of his descendant Jehoahaz, both of whose names connect the *ahaz* component with the specific divine name Yahweh—in the shortened forms of *yah* and *yeho* respectively—and accordingly mean 'Yahweh has seized', and both of whom are indeed seized by a divinely ordained act, although this is not said explicitly in the latter case). In the end, 'Ahaz slept with his ancestors, and they buried him in the city, in Jerusalem; but they did not bring him into the tombs of the kings of Israel. His son Hezekiah succeeded him' (2 Chron. 28.27).

● Hezekiah

The forty-sixth generation witnesses the reign of Hezekiah.
He is listed in the Davidic genealogy in 1 Chron. 3.13, and an
account of his reign is presented in 2 Chron. 29.1– 32.33.
That account begins as follows: 'Hezekiah was 25 years old
when he began to reign, and he reigned for 29 years in Jerusalem. His mother's name was Abijah daughter of Zechariah.
He did what was right in the sight of Yahweh, just as his ancestor David had done' (2 Chron. 29.1-2). The name 'Hezekiah'—which carries the meaning 'Yah [i.e. Yahweh] has
strengthened'—comes into significance in two episodes in his
story. The first is when King Sennacherib of Assyria invades
Judah, and King Hezekiah's response is to strengthen the for-
tifications of Jerusalem and to encourage his people with the
words, 'Be strong [the *hezek*- component of his name] and of
good courage; do not be afraid before the king of Assyria and
all the horde that is with him, for there is one greater with us
than with him. With him is an arm of flesh, but with us is our
god Yahweh [the *-iah* component of his name], to help us
and to fight our battles' (2 Chron. 32.7-8). The second reso-
nance with his designation as someone whom Yahweh has
strengthened comes sometime after the Assyrian threat has
been thwarted by Yahweh's intervention: 'In those days
Hezekiah became sick and was at the point of death; he
prayed to Yahweh, and he answered him and gave him a sign'
(2 Chron. 32.24), with the eventual outcome that 'Hezekiah
prospered in all his works' (v. 30). At the end, 'Hezekiah slept
with his ancestors, and they buried him on the ascent to the
tombs of the descendants of David; and all Judah and the
inhabitants of Jerusalem did him honour at his death. His son
Manasseh succeeded him' (v. 33).

● Manasseh

The forty-seventh generation witnesses the reign of Manasseh. He is listed in the Davidic genealogy in 1 Chron. 3.13, and an account of his reign is presented in 2 Chron. 33.1-20. We are told that 'Manasseh was 12 years old when he began to reign, and he reigned for 55 years in Jerusalem. He did what was evil in the sight of Yahweh, according to the abominable practices of the nations whom Yahweh drove out before the people of Israel. For he rebuilt the high places that his father Hezekiah had pulled down, and erected altars to the Baals, made sacred poles, worshipped all the host of heaven, and served them' (2 Chron. 33.1-3)—in other words, this man whose name means 'forgetting' (as is explained in Genesis 41.51, when the patriarch Joseph names his firstborn son Manasseh 'because the deity has made me forget all my hardship and all my father's house') has forgotten all the lessons that have been played out across the Annalists' canvas over many generations and not least in his father's generation. He will need to be reminded, and so we find that 'Yahweh spoke to Manasseh and to his people, but they gave no heed. Therefore Yahweh brought against them the commanders of the army of the king of Assyria, who took Manasseh captive in manacles, bound him with fetters, and brought him to Babylon. While he was in distress he entreated the favour of his god Yahweh and humbled himself greatly before the god of his fathers. He prayed to him, and the deity received his entreaty, heard his plea, and restored him again to Jerusalem and to his kingdom. Then Manasseh knew that Yahweh indeed was divine' (2 Chron. 33.10-13). He embarks on a new career of faithfulness, and is rewarded with a lengthy reign, after which 'Manasseh slept with his ancestors, and they buried him in his house. His son Amon succeeded him' (2 Chron. 33.20).

● Amon

The forty-eighth generation witnesses the reign of Amon. He is listed in the Davidic genealogy in 1 Chron. 3.14, and an account of his reign is presented in 2 Chron. 33.21-25: 'Amon was 22 years old when he began to reign, and he reigned for two years in Jerusalem. He did what was evil in the sight of Yahweh, as his father Manasseh had done. Amon sacrificed to all the images that his father Manasseh had made, and served them. He did not humble himself before Yahweh, as his father Manasseh had humbled himself, but this Amon incurred more and more guilt. His servants conspired against him and killed him in his house. But the people of the land killed all those who had conspired against King Amon; and the people of the land made his son Josiah king to succeed him.' That is the entire account in the Annals of Amon's brief reign, and it seems to belie the meaning of his name in Hebrew, which is 'craftsman' (so used in Proverbs 8.30's depiction of Wisdom as the Amon/craftsman at Yahweh's side during the creation of the world). More likely, then, in the context of the Annals is that we should think of this particular Israelite king's name in its Egyptian guise as the name of a certain deity, one which coincidentally happens to appear in a rather pertinent way in an Israelite oracle recorded in the book of Jeremiah: 'Yahweh of hosts, the god of Israel, has said: "See, I am bringing punishment upon Amon of Thebes, and Pharaoh, and Egypt and her gods and her kings, upon Pharaoh and upon those who trust in him. I will hand them over to those who seek their life"' (Jeremiah 46.25-26). In serving those non-Yahwistic images and not humbling himself before Yahweh, only to be killed by conspirators seeking his life, King Amon of Judah has fitted rather neatly into the pattern of that prophetic word from outside the Annals.

• Josiah

The forty-ninth generation witnesses the reign of Josiah. He is listed in the Davidic genealogy in 1 Chron. 3.14, and an account of his reign is presented in 2 Chron. 34.1– 35.27. That account begins as follows: 'Josiah was eight years old when he began to reign, and he reigned for 31 years in Jerusalem. He did what was right in the sight of Yahweh, and walked in the ways of his ancestor David' (2 Chron. 34.1-2). However, Josiah embarks on the disastrous policy of confronting Pharaoh Neco of Egypt, whereupon 'Neco sent envoys to him, saying, "What have I to do with you, king of Judah? I am not coming against you today, but against the house with which I am at war; and heaven has commanded me to hurry. Cease opposing the one who is with me, so that he will not destroy you." But Josiah would not turn away from him, but disguised himself in order to fight with him. He did not listen to the words of Neco from the mouth of the deity, but joined battle in the plain of Megiddo. The archers shot King Josiah; and the king said to his servants, "Take me away, for I am badly wounded". So his servants took him out of the chariot and carried him in his second chariot and brought him to Jerusalem. There he died, and was buried in the tombs of his ancestors' (2 Chron. 35.20-24). The story appears to contain a certain ironic spin on the king's name 'Josiah', for the name may well mean 'Yah [i.e. Yahweh] has healed', whereas in fact the deity does not heal him after he is left severely wounded by the archers, on account of his not having listened to the divine word that had been proclaimed to him by the pharaoh. The parallels with his ancestor Joash, whose name combines the same verbal element as that in Josiah but leaves the name of the deity unexpressed (simply 'he has healed') and whose fate is remarkably similar, are too marked to be entirely coincidental in the Annalists' story-world.

- **Johanan**

  Josiah's firstborn son is called 'Johanan' ('Yah[weh] has been gracious') in the genealogical list (3.15), and is brushed aside as the line of descent carries on through the second son, Jehoiakim (3.16-24). In the later telling of the tale (2 Chron. 36.1-3) he carries the more appropriate name of 'Jehoahaz' ('Yah[weh] has seized'). Nevertheless, so uninterested are the Annalists in his brief reign that they do not bother to give any account of the change of names in the way that they do for his brother Eliakim, a.k.a. 'Jehoiakim' (2 Chron. 36.4).

- **Jehoiakim**

  The fiftieth man to occupy the line of destiny is the second of Josiah's sons (3.15), but he is elevated to the throne in succession to his older brother (2 Chron. 36.3-4). The two forms of his name—'Jehoiakim' ('Yah[weh] raises up') and 'Eliakim' ('El raises up')—both express confidence in the divine choice of this ruler, but after an 11-year reign he is deposed by the Babylonian imperial authorities (2 Chron. 36.5-8). However, Jehoiakim has a young son (Jeconiah) through whom the Davidic line can continue beyond this catastrophe.

- **Zedekiah**

  In the turbulent last days of the kingdom of Judah, a time concerning which the Annalists accuse the Judahites of 'being exceedingly unfaithful, following all the abominations of the nations' (2 Chron. 36.14) and 'despising [Yahweh's] words and scoffing at his prophets, until Yahweh's wrath against his people became so great that there was no remedy' (v. 16), it is ironic that two members of the royal household—this man (1 Chron. 3.15) and his nephew (3.16)—bear a name which means 'Yah [i.e. Yahweh] is righteousness'.

- **Shallum**

  A fourth son of Josiah is listed by the Annalists (3.15). A certain fragment of Hebrew tradition may give this man a prominence that he doesn't have in the Annals (a prophetic oracle has come down to us claiming 'Thus says Yahweh concerning Shallum son of King Josiah of Judah, who succeeded his father Josiah, and who went away from this place: "He shall return here no more...and he shall never see this land again"' [Jeremiah 22.11-12]), but for the Annalists this character has only a marginal place in the grand scheme of things.

• Jeconiah

The fifty-first man to occupy the line of destiny carries two different names in the Annals: when first listed in the parade of the generations he is styled as 'Jeconiah' (3.16-17), but when it later comes to a description of his brief reign as king of Judah he is styled 'Jehoiachin' (2 Chron. 36.9). Readers are left to suppose that this is an analogous case to that of his father, concerning whom it is reported that 'the king of Egypt made...Eliakim king over Judah and Jerusalem and changed his name to Jehoiakim' (2 Chron. 36.4). But a name-change from 'Jeconiah ('Yah[weh] endures') to 'Jehoiachin' ('Yah-[weh] appoints') does the new eight-year-old king no good; he reigns for a mere 'three months and ten days in Jerusalem' before 'in the spring of the year King Nebuchadnezzar sent and brought him to Babylon, along with the precious vessels of the house of Yahweh, and made his brother Zedekiah king over Judah in Jerusalem' (2 Chron. 36.9-10).

• Zedekiah

Although Zedekiah is listed in second place in the genealogical citation of Jehoiakim's sons (3.16), when it comes to the telling of the tale he is said to have been '22 years old when he began to reign' (2 Chron. 36.11) after his brother was removed from the throne at the tender age of 'eight years old' (2 Chron. 36.9-10). This would appear to make Zedekiah the older brother by a considerable margin, yet the Annalists provide no explanation as to why the young child Jeconiah (a.k.a. 'Jehoiachin') rather than the young man Zedekiah should have succeeded to the throne on the death of their father Jehoiakim (a.k.a. 'Eliakim'). Perhaps some confusion has arisen on account of there being a Zedekiah also in the preceding generation, but in any event King Zedekiah's reign ends with the Babylonian sacking of Jerusalem (2 Chron. 36.17-19).

- **Shealtiel**

  Although a 'captive' (3.17), Jeconiah is able to father Shealtiel ('I have asked the deity') as the first of seven sons (3.18).

- **Malchiram**

  A name meaning 'my king is exalted' is an interesting choice for a captive former king to have bestowed upon his son.

- **Pedaiah**

  The fifty-second man to occupy the line of destiny carries the name 'Yah[weh] has ransomed'; there is a future beyond exile.

- **Shenazzar**

  A Babylonian-style name meaning 'may Sin [the moon god] protect the father' is another interesting name-choice.

- **Jekamiah**

  The exiled king returns to a traditional Hebrew name for his fifth son: 'Jekamiah' means 'Yah[weh] establishes'.

- **Hoshama**

  Persisting now with a Yahwistic theme in the naming of his sons, Jeconiah proclaims that 'Yah[weh] has heard'.

- **Nedabiah**

  In his final choice of name, the deposed king of Judah comes to the view that 'Yah[weh] has impelled'.

● Zerubbabel

The fifty-third man to occupy the line of destiny demonstrates in his very name the circumstances of his birth, for the final element 'babel' is in fact the city-name of Babylon and the whole name probably means something like 'offspring of Babylon'. Since his grandfather Jeconiah (a.k.a. 'Jehoiachin') had been taken into captivity in Babylon by King Nebuchadnezzar (2 Chron. 36.10) and his father Pedaiah was a son of 'Jeconiah the captive' (1 Chron. 3.17-18), the context from which this new child emerges is clearly implied. What is not clear in the Annals, since they come to a close with the open-ended possibilities of the decree of King Cyrus of Persia (2 Chron. 36.23), is whether Zerubbabel comes out of Babylon back to the land where his grandfather had reigned so briefly some 80 years before (2 Chron. 36.9-11, 21). Certain other traditions suggest that he did—but they also suggest that his father was Shealtiel rather than Pedaiah (Haggai 1.1).

● Shimei

Alongside the man who carries the mark of Babylonian exile in his name stands someone whose presence seems to hark back to pre-exilic times, for Shimei is a solid Hebrew name ('he [i.e. the deity] has heard') which echoes throughout the tribes of Israel in the Annalists' lists. A man named Shimei had been the founder of one of the subdivisions of families of Levites (6.17, further itemized in 23.7-11), and another had been one of the chief officials involved in Hezekiah's reforms (2 Chron. 31.12-13); several other levitical families also made use of the name (1 Chron. 6.29, 42; 25.3, 17; 2 Chron. 29.14). There had also been a prominent Shimei among the Simeonites (1 Chron. 4.26-27) and another among the Reubenites (5.4). Thus the appearance of such a name at the end of the Babylonian captivity is a reassuring sign.

- ● **Meshullam**

  Once again a firstborn son will turn out not to be the one through whom the legacy is passed on.

- ● **Hananiah**

  The fifty-fourth man to occupy the line of destiny carries the name 'Yah [i.e. Yahweh] has been gracious' (3.19).

- ● **Shelomith**

  One of just a few occasions—such as in David's and Solomon's generations—on which the Annalists list a 'sister' (3.19).

- ● **Hashubah**

  After the listing of a daughter, a further five sons are added to Zerubbabel's account, beginning with Hashubah (3.20).

- ● **Ohel**

  A name meaning 'tent' (so used, for example, in 15.1: 'he pitched a tent') seems a strange one to bestow upon a child.

- ● **Berechiah**

  'Yah[weh] has blessed' returns to the more profound theme that had been evident in the naming of Hananiah above.

- ● **Hasadiah**

  'Yah[weh] has shown loyalty/kindness' continues the theme, and perhaps indicates a feeling about the end of exile.

- ● **Jushab-hesed**

  In his final choice of name, Zerubbabel proclaims, 'May kindness/loyalty be returned' (3.20).

• Pelatiah

The fifty-fifth generation has just one name to bring forward (3.21)—though the NRSV suggests otherwise by rendering the beginning of the verse as 'The sons of Hananiah: Pelatiah and Jeshaiah'. The latter name, however, is not to be taken as designating a brother of Pelatiah, but rather his son (see the comments on this matter under 'Jeshaiah' on the next page). Thus Pelatiah stands alone in the sequence of generations. His name, on the other hand, is not unique in the Annals, for there is an incident recorded elsewhere in the genealogies regarding '500 men of the Simeonites' who, under the leadership of a certain Pelatiah and his three brothers, 'went to Mount Seir' and 'destroyed the remnant of the Amalekites that had escaped' (4.42-43). The name carries the meaning 'Yah [i.e. Yahweh] has delivered', so it might be thought to make a fitting designation for an Israelite fighting man. In the case of the latter-day Pelatiah it could denote, as a number of other names around this section of the chart appear to do, a particular feeling about the end of the captivity in Babylon, yet the Annalists only set out the names and do not relate any stories about them. The scroll of Nehemiah happens to list a Pelatiah among 'the leaders of the people' who attended the sealing of the covenant after the rebuilding of the walls of Jerusalem (Nehemiah 10.22), but it is not at all clear that that man—almost hidden within a crowd of 44 elders—is the same individual as the Davidic descendant brought forward by the Annalists to stand in the line of destiny.

3:21

might be son of Hananiah

• Jeshaiah

✗

but it will be later interpreter

The fifty-sixth generation is represented solely by a man named Jeshaiah (3.21). As mentioned in the introductory comments to this genealogical chart, the received Hebrew text at the point of 3.21 has a slight infelicity which has caused a number of readers to suppose that the Annalists regard Jeshaiah as the brother rather than the son of Pelatiah, but since the infelicitous formulation is not in keeping with the rest of the dynastic chart, and runs against the reading of the venerable Greek, Syriac and Latin versions (together with certain other Hebrew manuscripts), it is best to understand the verse in question as presenting Jeshaiah as indeed the son and not the brother of Pelatiah. As the son, then, he carries the Davidic line into a new generation, and in turn passes the mantle of inheritance on to his own son Rephaiah. He is not the only one to bear this particular name in the Annals, for we read of a Jeshaiah who receives the eighth allocation among the Asaphite musicians in the time of King David (25.15) and of another who inherits the task of overseeing the temple treasuries (26.25). We also meet the name later in the Annals in a slightly longer form (the Hebrew spelling *yeshayahu* rather than *yeshayah*) in the guise of 'the prophet Isaiah' (2 Chron. 26.22; 32.20, 32); in either form, it carries the meaning 'Yah [i.e. Yahweh] has saved'. That had been a particularly relevant name for the episode in which 'King Hezekiah and the prophet Isaiah son of Amoz prayed because of [Sennacherib's invasion of Judah] and cried to heaven, and Yahweh sent an angel who cut off all the mighty warriors and commanders and officers in the camp of the king of Assyria, so he returned with disgrace to his own land' (2 Chron. 32.20-21). Thus it can function as an auspicious name again in the time after the Babylonian captivity.

no patronage given

● **Rephaiah**

The fifty-seventh generation is represented solely by a man named Rephaiah (3.21). As was the case with the name of his grandfather, Pelatiah (and will also be the case with the name of a later descendant, Neariah), this character-designation happens to appear in a particular incident recorded elsewhere in the genealogies: 'And some of them, 500 men of the Simeonites, went to Mount Seir, having as their leaders Pelatiah, Neariah, Rephaiah, and Uzziel, sons of Ishi; they destroyed the remnant of the Amalekites that had escaped, and they have lived there to this day' (4.42-43); the incident is said to have occurred 'in the days of King Hezekiah of Judah' (4.41). There is also a Rephaiah listed as one of the 'mighty warriors of their generations' and 'heads of their ancestral houses' in the tribe of Issachar (7.2), so perhaps the name resonates with heroic status and is thus a fitting designation for a man who leads the house of David on into the future that awaits it. The meaning of the name is not entirely clear, but if it carries the meaning 'Yah[weh] has healed/restored' (which a slightly different spelling in the Hebrew—namely the inclusion of the quiescent letter *aleph*—would clarify) then it sits well in a sequence preceded by his father Jeshaiah ('Yah[weh] has saved') and grandfather Pelatiah ('Yah[weh] has delivered').

• Arnan

The fifty-eighth generation is represented solely by a man named Arnan (3.21). Unlike the names that occur around it in this line of descent from David, this particular character-designation is unique; that is to say, there are no other individuals with this name anywhere else in the Annals, neither in the genealogies of chs. 1– 9 nor in the later stories (and neither does it appear, for that matter, in any other document that has been incorporated into the Hebrew Bible). In a certain sense, however, it does make an appearance in the Annalists' story of King David, where a character named 'Ornan' (spelled in Hebrew with precisely the same letters as 'Arnan', though vocalized differently in the reading tradition) is encountered: 'Then the angel of Yahweh commanded Gad to tell David that he should go up and erect an altar to Yahweh on the threshing-floor of Ornan the Jebusite' (21.18). The king goes up and, after protracted negotiations with the man, 'David paid Ornan 600 shekels of gold by weight for the site, and built there an altar to Yahweh and presented burnt offerings and offerings of well-being' (21.25-26). And in due course David's successor Solomon sets about 'to build the house of Yahweh in Jerusalem on Mount Moriah, where Yahweh had appeared to his father David, at the place that David had designated, on the threshing-floor of Ornan the Jebusite' (2 Chron. 3.1). Thus we might say that the name, in identically written but differently pronounced forms (although the different vocalization might not reflect any desire on the part of the Annalists themselves to create such a distinction), occurs both in the Annalists' story of how David came to designate the site for the temple and in their table of Davidic descendants who might re-establish the temple-centred kingdom of their ancestor.

● Obadiah

The fifty-ninth generation is represented solely by a man named Obadiah (3.21). Carrying as it does the meaning 'servant of Yah[weh]', this is a popular name within these genealogical lists and also in the later stories related by the Annalists. In the lists we meet an Obadiah among the chiefs of the tribe of Issachar (7.3), two others—or rather one twice-mentioned—among the leading families of the tribe of Benjamin (8.38; 9.44), and another among the first group of Levites to return to Jerusalem after the Babylonian captivity (9.16). In the stories we encounter an Obadiah who was the second of the 'mighty and experienced warriors, expert with shield and spear, whose faces were like the faces of lions and who were swift as gazelles on the mountains', who 'went over to David at the stronghold in the wilderness' (12.8-9); another who appears to have been the leader of the Zebulunites in the time of David (if he preceded his son Ishmaiah in office: 27.19); another who goes out with his fellow officials to teach 'the book of the law of Yahweh...through all the cities of Judah' in the time of King Hezekiah (2 Chron. 17.7-9); and yet another who is appointed as one of the levitical overseers of the temple repairs in the time of King Josiah (2 Chron. 34.12). Each of these personages blessed with the name of Obadiah is spoken of with approval by the Annalists; one can well imagine that they regarded the designation 'Servant of Yahweh' as a very fitting one too for a descendant of David standing on the line of destiny that was moving ever forward.

● Shecaniah

The sixtieth generation is represented solely by a man named
Shecaniah (3.21). Although this name is not as ubiquitous in
the Annals as the name listed in the previous generation, it
nevertheless does appear outside of the Davidic genealogy.
Among the 'officers of the sanctuary', who 'had as their appointed duty in their service to enter the house of Yahweh
according to the procedure established for them by their
ancestor Aaron, as Yahweh the god of Israel had commanded
him' (24.5, 19), 'the tenth lot fell to Shecaniah' (24.11). Later,
in the time of King Hezekiah, there is another Shecaniah
among the 'faithful assistants' of the Keeper of the Offerings,
working 'in the cities of the priests, to distribute the portions
to their kindred, old and young alike, by divisions, except
those enrolled by genealogy, males from three years old and
upwards, all who entered the house of Yahweh as the duty of
each day required, for their service according to their offices,
by their divisions—for the enrolment of the priests was according to their ancestral houses, and that of the Levites from
20 years old and upwards was according to their offices, by
their divisions' (2 Chron. 31.15-17). In such an elaborate system regarding 'all who entered the house of Yahweh', a man
called Shecaniah—a name that carries the meaning 'Yah [i.e.
Yahweh] has taken up his abode'—is perfectly cast. But so
too can the name do good service as designating the heir to
the seat of David, that mighty monarch who had put all things
in readiness for Yahweh to take up his abode in the very
'house of Yahweh' that would be built by a son of David on
the site prepared for it.

● **Shemaiah**

The sixty-first generation is represented solely by a man named Shemaiah (3.22). This name is reasonably widespread in the Annals, appearing among both the Simeonites (4.37) and the Reubenites (5.4), and several times among the Levites (15.8; 26.4), including 'the scribe Shemaiah son of Nethanel, a Levite, [who] recorded [the falling of the lots] in the presence of the king and the officers' and other eminent persons (24.6). But arguably the most significant character given this name is the one who comes onto the scene twice during the reign of King Rehoboam. On the first occasion we encounter him, the Annalists relate that 'the word of Yahweh came to the godly man Shemaiah: Say to King Rehoboam of Judah, son of Solomon, and to all Israel in Judah and Benjamin: "Thus says Yahweh: You shall not go up or fight against your kindred"' (2 Chron. 11.2-4). Then in a second incident, 'the prophet Shemaiah came to Rehoboam and the officers of Judah, who had gathered at Jerusalem because of Shishak, and said to them, "Thus says Yahweh: You abandoned me, so I have abandoned you to the hand of Shishak"' (2 Chron. 12.5). What is noticeable about both of these episodes is the reaction of the king and his people: on the first occasion, 'they heeded the word of Yahweh and turned back from the expedition against Jeroboam' (2 Chron. 11.4), and on the subsequent occasion they 'humbled themselves and said, "Yahweh is in the right"' (2 Chron. 12.6). This 'heeding/hearing the word of Yahweh' is the appropriately matching behaviour to the character designated 'Shemaiah'—a name which carries the meaning 'Yah [i.e. Yahweh] has heard/heeded' (indeed it uses the same Hebrew verb as does the phrase just mentioned)—and perhaps augurs well for the Davidic descendant upon whom the same name is bestowed.

- **Hattush**

  The first of Shemaiah's sons (3.22) is presumably the same man as the Hattush mentioned in Ezra 8.2-3.

- **Igal**

  A name meaning 'he [i.e. the deity] redeems', once borne by one of the twelve legendary spies of Israel (Numbers 13.7).

- **Bariah**

  A name meaning 'fleeing' or 'fugitive' (related to the verb 'to flee' which occurs in 2 Chron. 10.2).

- **Neariah**

  The sixty-second man to occupy the line of destiny (3.22) bears a name meaning 'Yah's [i.e. Yahweh's] lad'.

- **Shaphat**

  A name meaning 'he [i.e. the deity] has judged', analogous to the earlier name Jehoshaphat, 'Yah[weh] has judged'.

- **(anonymous)**

  It is stated that Shemaiah had 'six' sons in all (3.22). Either a name has fallen from the list or the number should be 'five'.

- ## Elioenai

  The sixty-third man to occupy the line of destiny carries a name that means 'my eyes are toward my god' (3.23). It is a name that occurs with honour in the Annalists' list of Simeonite clans (4.36 [v. 48: 'these mentioned by name were leaders in their families, and their clans increased greatly']) as well as in the list of Benjaminite families (7.8 [v. 9: 'their enrolment by genealogies, according to their generations, as heads of their ancestral houses']), and now it stands in the penultimate position on the central line of descent.

- ## Hizkiah

  This generation also sees a reprise in the Davidic family line of an auspicious name ('Yah[weh] has strenthened') that had been carried in the forty-sixth generation by one of the Judahite kings in the slightly variant form of 'Hezekiah' (*chizkiyahu* in comparison with *chizkiyah* here). That king was one of the ones with whom the Annalists were most impressed (note 2 Chron. 31.20), but this latter-generation prince of the house of David amounts to nothing, at least insofar as the central line proceeds through another man.

- ## Azrikam

  The youngest brother at this penultimate stage of the parade of generations also reprises a name found elsewhere in the Annals, although under much less favourable circumstances than his older brothers' names. 'Azrikam, the commander of the palace' is one of three key Judahite individuals (including the crown prince) killed in a war between the two Israelite kingdoms during the time of King Ahaz (2 Chron. 28.7). The irony of that situation is that the name Azrikam means 'my help has arisen'.

● **Anani and his brothers**

The sixty-fourth generation stands potentially on the cusp of a new era, in the schematization of the Annalists. The seven sons of Elioenai stand before us—Hodaviah, Eliashib, Pelaiah, Akkub, Johanan, Delaiah and Anani (3.24)—but which one will carry on the Davidic legacy? At the thirty-second generation had stood Jesse, who became the father of the great David and who accordingly was honoured in the rallying cry, 'We are yours, O David, and with you, O son of Jesse!' (12.18). Prophetic traditions in Israel would have it that at a destined time 'a shoot shall come out from the stump of Jesse, and a branch shall grow out of his roots' (Isaiah 11.1). The anticipation is intense: one of these seven men in the second thirty-second generation could become the father of the New David, ushering in a renewal in the nation's destiny, and a return to its golden age as envisaged by the Annalists. Would the next generation be singing, 'We are with you, O son of Hodaviah'? Perhaps the centrally placed Akkub could turn out to be the father of the anticipated one? Or might it be the youngster Anani who in time would carry the line forward, just as David himself was the youngest of his brothers when 'Yahweh, the god of Israel, chose [him] from all [his] ancestral house' (28.4)? But we hear no triumphant shouts; only silence. The parade has passed before us in uninterrupted procession all the way down the line from the very beginning with Adam so many generations before, but here it comes to an end, with no further footsteps to be heard after Anani. The Annals are poised, pointing forward into a hoped-for future, and in doing so they have become frozen in time, a time capsule sealed at Generation 64.

David
(1 Chronicles 10–29)

1 Chronicles 10–12: David's Elevation to his Throne

Chapter 10

Having exhaustively catalogued the generations, the Annalists launch somewhat abruptly into their main narrative with the words 'Now the Philistines fought against Israel' (10.1). 'The Philistines' had been mentioned very early on in the genealogies of the nations, in 1.12, where the list of peoples said to be descended from the eponymous Egypt included 'Casluhim, out of whom the Philistines came' (though the NRSV prefers to link them with 'Caphtorim', in view of Hebrew prophetic traditions that do so, to be seen in Amos 9.7 and Jeremiah 47.4). Thus the Philistines are said to be Africans (Hamites), descendants of the Hamitic Egypt. Whether 'coming out of Casluhim' is meant to tell us that they do not belong in the land of Israel, but have come from somewhere else, is open to question in this account. The expression may just mean that they are descendants of such-and-such a people with no implications about movements of peoples across the lands, but the possibility is there that we are to think of the Philistines as having 'come out' from an Hamitic land and now appearing in the land of Israel fighting against the Israelites for control of this rightfully Shemitic land. Nothing is said explicitly about such matters, but ironically there will be later references to the people of Israel having 'come out of [the land of] Egypt' (e.g. 2 Chron. 5.10 and 6.5), which may suggest that the picture is rather of Israelites coming into this land and seeking to wrest control of it from the already-settled Philistines.

The Annalists' picture may rather be simply that fighting is endemic to humankind, and so there is no real need for a more detailed explanation as to why two peoples are fighting over the same land. Everyone fights; it is simply the natural order of things. The genealogical listings in the preceding chapters of the Annals had already presented horrid vignettes of fighting, where various tribes of Israelites fought against diverse peoples, such as the Simeonites who 'attacked the Meunites…and exterminated them…and settled in their place, because there was pasture there for their flocks' (4.41) or the Reubenites who 'made war on the Hagrites…and [having massacred them] lived in their tents throughout all the region east of Gilead' (5.10). The image has thus already been created of Israelites flexing their muscles and tussling with other peoples for pieces of territory. As the story unfolds, there will be many more battles without particular explanation, but before one of them we will meet an intriguing phrase: 'In the spring of the year, the time when kings go out to battle, Joab led out the army, ravaged the country of the Ammonites, and came and besieged Rabbah' (20.1). It seems to be a case of 'Spring is here; let's go out and fight somebody!'. It is apparently assumed in this story-world that going out to fight is the natural way of things. Hence our storytellers do not feel the need to give a special reason or explanation for a particular war or battle.

So here we find the Philistines fighting against the Israelites. This will more or less continue throughout the Annals, in point of fact. Even in 2 Chron. 28.18 there is a reference to the continuing need to fight the Philistines. Thus even at that time, which is the reign of Ahaz the father of Hezekiah, these pesky Philistines are still getting in the road of the Israelites. That verse says, 'and the Philistines had made raids on the cities in the Shephelah and the Negeb of Judah, and had taken Beth-shemesh, Aijalon, Gederoth, Soco with its villages, Timnah with its villages, and Gimzo with its villages; and they settled there. For Yahweh brought Judah low because of King Ahaz of Israel, for he had behaved without restraint in Judah and had been faithless to Yahweh.' So there the hint is that the Philistines are still a threat because the king of the time was unfaithful (a note that echoes throughout the story). But as the David story unfolds, we will see that this particular king will be eminently successful against these Philistines.

However, at this initial point, before David comes on the scene, there is no success against the Philistines. In fact, as 10.1 says, 'the men of Israel fled before the Philistines'. This is reiterated in v. 7, in that when the people 'saw that the army had fled…they abandoned their towns and fled'. So at the moment when we first have details of the Israelite–Philistine conflict, the Philistines are in the driving seat. The Israelites are fallen in front of them. Indeed the word 'fall' is also reiterated throughout this episode: in v. 1 'the men of Israel…fell slain on Mount Gilboa'; in v. 4 'Saul fell on his sword'; in v. 5 'his armour-bearer fell on his sword'. In such an all-encompassing manner Israel falls before the Philistine onslaught.

In particular, and almost as soon as the story proper has begun, we encounter the fall of Saul. Although he had been given double-billing in the genealogies (at 8.33 and 9.39), little is said of this character, who serves merely as an inadequate antecedent to the hero David. Not until 11.2 does anyone refer to him, and then only grudgingly, as having been 'king', although that is perhaps anticipated by the narrative reference to 'the kingdom' in 10.14. Thus readers can think of him as a kind of quasi-king of Israel, but the storyline gives him no time to settle into a proper reign. 'The battle pressed hard on Saul' (v. 3), 'and the archers found him, and he was wounded by the archers'. Actually the Hebrew text uses two different but closely related words for 'archers' in its terse description of this dramatic event, so perhaps there are two slightly different kinds of specialist soldiers involved in the detection and liquidation of the opposing commander-in-chief. But the important thing is that Saul is wounded. And it may be too that part of his horrid end is to have witnessed the death of his three sons, since it is recorded first in v. 2 that 'the Philistines overtook Saul and his sons; and the Philistines killed Jonathan and Abinadab and Malchishua, sons of Saul'; this is said before Saul is wounded, so it may be that we are to think of him seeing his sons killed before he comes to his own end.

As in the case of the name 'Saul' itself, readers were introduced twice to these sons' names in the genealogies. In 8.33 and 9.39 the sons of Saul were listed, though in a slightly different order and with a fourth son as well, one who is not mentioned here, namely Eshbaal. Perhaps we are to suppose that one branch of Saul's family (as represented by the fighting men of his household) survives this battle. If so, then v. 6 takes that away from us, because it says, 'thus Saul died; he and his three sons and all his house died together'. But there is a discrepancy between this statement and the list in the genealogy of Saul, which goes on for another 12 generations after Saul. Thus the Annalists first of all said that Saul's house survived for at least 12 generations, but now they say that 'all his house died together'. Perhaps 'all his house died together' means not that every single member of Saul's family was killed, but that the dynasty of Saul, or the possibility of there being a royal line continuing on from him, was what really perished on that fateful day on Mount Gilboa. Perhaps there is something about son Number Four or about the line of the family as represented earlier that meant they could not hold the throne now that Saul and these three sons are killed. There is no turning back from this cataclysmic event.

Matters are underlined by the repetition of the words 'dead' and 'died' (forms of the Hebrew verb *mut*) in vv. 5-7: 'When his armour-bearer saw that Saul was *dead*, he also fell on his sword and *died*; thus Saul *died*— he and his three sons and all his house *died* together—and when all the men of Israel…saw…that Saul and his sons were *dead*, they abandoned their towns and fled'. Thus there is no getting away from the finality and thoroughgoing nature of this defeat. But even so, this total end of the house of Saul is a beginning for our storytellers. This is the first real story that they tell, and it leads to the new beginning with David, a story that would arguably not have been possible if the character of Saul were not moved out of the way first.

Notice Saul's fear about the Philistines: that they will 'come and make sport' of him (v. 4). It is not entirely clear what 'make sport' means in the light of the reference to them being 'uncircumcised'. Saul himself is presumably circumcised, being an Israelite. Perhaps also, in the light of certain imagery here with the 'sword' and the 'thrusting through', some notion of the sexual abuse of those defeated in battle may be in view. This is the only place in these Annals that the practice of circumcision (or rather, strictly speaking, the non-practice of circumcision) is referred to, with the implication that the Israelites can be distinguished from the Philistines in that Israelites circumcise themselves while Philistines do not indulge in such a practice. Saul will be stripped of his clothes and other valuables (as happens in v. 8), and this mark of difference may become a matter of ridicule by the enemy soldiers.

When the Philistines come to the aftermath of the battle, they indeed find 'Saul and his sons fallen' (v. 8). Israel, in fact, is fallen. The victors take Saul's head (v. 9), and the symbolism in this gruesome action is quite obvious: Saul had been the head of the Israelite people, and now the enemies of Israel take the head of the head away, and fasten that head in the temple of their god Dagon (v. 10). One could hardly imagine a worse end to the reign of a king of Israel, somebody who is a devotee of Yahweh, that his head is put on a stake or nailed up on a wall in the temple of a rival deity. It might be thought by some to be a symbol that Dagon had defeated Yahweh, but that is not the interpretation that the Annalists want us to have. In fact they may see this as a fitting end to Saul's career, that he should have his head in the temple of Dagon because he did not have his heart with Yahweh, according to what is said in v. 13.

Why did Saul die? In this story-world there is no analysis of whether he was a poor military strategist or whether he was simply outnumbered by the Philistine troops against him, and there is certainly no analysis of whether the mighty fighter David (who is said in 11.2 to have been 'commanding the army of Israel even while Saul was king') ought to have been at the battle helping the king of Israel. No blame will be attached to David in any of this. No, Saul has the blame himself, according to the Annalists: 'Saul died for his unfaithfulness; he was unfaithful to Yahweh' (v. 13). It is as simple as that, and thus it is quite right that his head should appear in front of Dagon. 'Unfaithfulness' is a key word in these Annals. We met it already in 9.1, even before the grand narrative of Israel's life under the Davidic dynasty gets underway. It is said (in 9.1) that 'all Israel was enrolled by genealogies, and these are written in the Book of the Kings of Israel; and Judah was taken into exile in Babylon because of their unfaithfulness'. The destiny of the people, the direction of the story, is noted: because of Israel's unfaithfulness, they will be taken into exile. In a sense, then, Saul here, with his head taken into 'exile' to the Philistine territory, is a paradigm or prototype for the people as a whole. Under David's faithfulness, and the faithfulness of certain of his descendants who reign after him, all will be well, but in the end the unfaithfulness even of descendants of David, and the people led astray by them, will cause everything to be undone. In 2 Chron. 36.13-14 the lead-in to the period of exile is phrased in this way: 'He [King Zedekiah] stiffened his neck and hardened his heart against turning to Yahweh, the god of Israel; all the leading priests and the people also were exceedingly unfaithful, following all the abominations of the nations, and they polluted the house of Yahweh that he had consecrated in Jerusalem'. Israel's god tried to turn them from that, but to no avail, and so he took them all off to Babylon. Saul here already in the story of his unfaithfulness gives us the picture.

Even so, no details are given in story form of Saul's unfaithfulness. It is simply said that 'he did not keep the command of Yahweh'. We are not told what that 'command' (or 'word', Hebrew *davar*) was as such, but we are told that 'moreover, he had consulted a medium, seeking guidance, and did not seek guidance from Yahweh'. There is a play-on-words here, in that in Hebrew the name 'Saul' is from the verb *sha'al*, meaning 'to ask' (his name *sha'ul* is in the form of a passive participle, the one who is 'asked for' or really wanted by his family or people), and here he is said to have 'asked/consulted' a medium—Saul had 'sauled' a medium. The character whose very name implies that he had been 'asked for', ends up asking questions in the wrong place, seeking guidance from a medium rather than from the prophets of Yahweh.

The Annalists do not reveal why Saul might have done such a thing; they simply make it abundantly clear that in their view he ought not to have done it. There is more to the play-on-words, though, than simply that Saul 'sauled' a medium, because the form of the verb fashioned by the Annalists to depict the consultation of the medium is the infinitive construct, which is *she'ol*. A medium is of course somebody who is thought to be in contact with the world of the dead, the realm known in Hebrew as 'Sheol'. This shadowy underworld is referred to in various ancient Hebrew stories (such as the patriarch Jacob's cry that 'I shall go down to Sheol to my son, mourning' in Genesis 37.35) and songs (such as the psalmist's rhetorical questions 'Who can live and never see death? Who can escape the power of Sheol?' in Psalm 89.48). It is not generally brought into the Annalists' story-world, but its appearance here at 1 Chron. 10.13 makes for a very clever double play-on-words: Saul has not only 'sauled' but has 'sheoled' this unnamed medium; he looked to the realm of the dead to give him guidance, instead of to the heavenly realm, to Yahweh—and 'therefore Yahweh put him to death' (v. 14)! He who had sought Sheol, goes to Sheol.

'Seeking Yahweh' would seem to be another concept of significance for the Annalists. In 28.9 David is presented as giving prominence to this notion, as the most important advice that he has to pass on to his son and successor Solomon. That section may be thought of as the central section of the Annals (i.e. of 1 and 2 Chronicles taken together as one book), and that idea may be regarded as the pivotal idea in the book: 'And you, my son Solomon, know the god of your father, and serve him with single mind and willing heart, for Yahweh searches every mind, and understands every plan and thought; if you seek him, he will be found by you, but if you forsake him, he will abandon you forever'. It is noticeable throughout what we call '2 Chronicles' that this scheme comes out again and again: kings that seek Yahweh are rewarded, being given success, health, long life, victory over their enemies and all the good things a Hebrew tradent might imagine, whereas kings that forsake Yahweh die young or suffer defeat in battle or disease in their body or have some other mark of judgment placed upon them. Thus already here Saul again sets the paradigm: he did not seek Yahweh, and so he dies—and not just he, but his whole house is cut off from Israel.

The bodies of Saul and his sons are brought to Jabesh and are buried under the oak there (v. 12). As it happens, the Hebrew word 'Jabesh' (*yavesh*) means 'dry', and is used in a prophetic utterance recorded in the book of Ezekiel in which dry bones that have no flesh on them serve as an image of the death of Israel. Here in a sense Saul's bones being buried in this dry place, this Jabesh site, is perhaps equally a symbol for the death or lack of life in Israel, although the Annalists will not dwell long on such an image. It is also worthy of note that the head of Saul had been taken away by and presumably remains with the Philistines; it is his body that the warriors of Jabesh are able to bury. The head of Israel's quasi-king is not mentioned again. David will later achieve success over the Philistines, but he does not bring back Saul's head. The house of Saul will never again rule Israel; that 'head' is now out of the way, and the scene is set for David to be elevated to the throne.

Chapter 11

The unparalleled David now enters the picture. He is at Hebron and the people of Israel are gathering—in fact it is said that no less than 'all Israel gathered together to David' (11.1). Only 'all Jabesh-gilead' had been involved in giving a decent burial to Saul and his sons (10.11-12), but 'all

Israel' is involved in acknowledging David as the new king. With one voice they say to David, 'See, we are your bone and your flesh', a delicious little irony in view of the 'bones' without flesh (10.12) of Saul and his sons that have been buried. But of course 'your bone and your flesh' is an expression for intimate relationship, as in Genesis 2.23 when Eve is brought to Adam and he exclaims 'This at last is bone of my bones and flesh of my flesh!' Thus it is indicated that, at least as far as these writers are concerned, David is the quintessential Israelite and all Israel is for him.

Indeed it seems in v. 2 that even while Saul was notionally ruling, David was already the hero. We might then ask why David was not leading the Israelite forces at Mount Gilboa—even worse, it appears from a later narrative aside (in 12.19) that he was prepared to fight on the opposing side—but none of the gathered Israelites ask such a question. They rather express complete assurance that Yahweh wants David to be 'the shepherd of [his] people Israel' and to be 'the ruler over [his] people Israel'. The image of the king as a shepherd is a common one in Hebrew tradition (as represented in various prophetic passages such as Ezekiel 34.1-24 and Zechariah 11.3-17), and in point of fact certain other Hebrew storytelling traditions may take the image literally and depict the mighty David as having once been a humble shepherd-boy (somewhat in the style of the prophet Amos, who is said to have proclaimed that 'Yahweh took me from following the flock' [Amos 7.15]), but the Annalists have no time for such stories. They present a David who suddenly stands fully formed as a regal personage, using the shepherding motif as an image of him as the one who will guide and protect his people. By implication Saul was unable to do that.

Without further ado David is 'anointed king over Israel' by 'all the elders of Israel' (v. 3), this anointing being carried out 'according to the word of Yahweh by Samuel'. No details are given concerning this 'word of Yahweh' that came by means of Samuel, and indeed no stories are told about the figure of Samuel as such. The name is mentioned once or twice by the Annalists simply as a prophet or seer who was around at the time. Here they are satisfied merely to say that it is the divine will that David be anointed king.

Immediately the storytellers relocate David from Hebron to the city that will become the centre of the tale: 'David and all Israel marched to Jerusalem' (v. 4). The reader is given a small note that that city 'is Jebus, where the Jebusites were, the inhabitants of the land'. The same expression 'the inhabitants of the land' appears again towards the end of the David story in 22.18, when the victorious monarch rejoices that 'Yahweh has delivered the inhabitants of the land into my hand, and the land is subdued before Yahweh and his people'; thus it would seem that here at the beginning of the story, reference is being made to a non-Israelite or non-Yahwistic group that must be overcome. However, there might also be for the Annalists something of the notion of displacing Saul, that non-seeker of Yahweh (10.14), since their genealogies had listed Saul's family as living in Jerusalem (8.32; 9.38). Either there is a discrepancy between the genealogy's depiction of Benjaminites, including Saul's family, living in Jerusalem and this later statement concerning 'the inhabitants of the land' living in Jerusalem, or there is something of a deliberate echo here to what has just been told about the demise of Saul's family; that is, in this matter, too, the house of David displaces the house of Saul. Jerusalem had seemingly been Saul's city, but now David will make it his.

He is not put off by the words of the present occupants. They may be confidently boasting, 'You won't get in here!', or they may be desperately imploring, 'Do not come in here!' (the Hebrew construction *lo tavo hennah* in v. 5 is capable of either nuance), but either way their words are of no avail, for it seems that no sooner have they been uttered than David has taken 'the stronghold of Zion' and the place has been re-branded as 'the city of David'. We are not told quite how he manages to break into this fortress, but he will never be dislodged from his position of strength and power once he is in this city and builds it all around him (v. 8). He is now at the centre of a new centralized government, under-pinned by military power, of course, but with the consent of 'all Israel', according to the Annalists. Once again in v. 10 we are told that 'all Israel' wanted David to be made king, in accordance with Yahweh's word (re-iterating v. 3). It is all a preordained plan by Yahweh, and it is all carried through with the full consent of absolutely everybody.

So what had been Jebus becomes 'the city of David'. At a stroke—a master-stroke—everything has been changed, and nothing will ever be quite the same again. Jerusalem will not look back; it will now be a new glorious capital where Yahweh himself will be in residence. But notice the residency has changed: from 'the inhabitants of the land' (v. 4) and 'the inhabitants of Jebus' (v. 5) to 'David' (who now 'inhabits' the place in v. 7, using the same Hebrew verb as had been used concerning the earlier residents). David now resides where previously there had been other inhabitants. Not long before in the narrative there had been mention of the Philistines inhabiting the cities from which the men of Israel had fled (10.7); thus it can be seen that already David is reversing what happened before. The Philistines had been successful against Saul and had been taking over where Israelites had lived; now David is being successful and is taking over where non-Israelites (or at best failed Israelites) had lived.

Readers cannot fail to notice that clusters of 'threes' and 'thirties' occur over and over in the latter parts of ch. 11. The first such figure appears in 11.11, a figure of 'thirty' (*shloshim*) according to the received Hebrew text, but it ought to be read as 'three' (*shloshah*) according to the NRSV. It seems that there is a legendary group of special warriors, perhaps a triumvirate of especially mighty men around David. Perhaps, though, this group is 'The Thirty', as a military band of some kind designated by a certain number, similar to the expressions 'the thousands and the hundreds' (13.1), that is, a round figure used as a means of designating a particular organizational structure: military troops arranged into divisions and companies. A troop designated as 'a hundred' might not consist precisely of 100 soldiers, just as a Roman *centurion* might not necessarily have 100 people in his troop; so similarly the number of 'a thousand' that appears many times in these Annals may be, rather than denoting literally a troop of 1000 men, merely a designation for a larger cohort or division of soldiers, and 'a thirty' might be a designation for a smaller cohort or company of soldiers.

In any case the Annalists present here some vignettes of heroic deeds done by certain mighty men among the warriors of David. It is a little repetitious, since what is recorded concerning the mighty warrior Jashobeam in v. 11 is replicated in regard to the equally mighty warrior Abishai in v. 20; both individuals are said to have been chief of a particular group and both were reputed to have despatched with his spear some 300 enemy soldiers. This could be taken to mean that three divisions (three 'hundreds') of opposing forces were defeated by one smaller company (one 'thirty') of David's men. But perhaps the Annalists want us to believe that one man was able—or rather that two different men on two different occasions were able—single-handedly to overcome far superior numbers of the enemy. That may well be so, but in among all this an important thing to notice is in v. 13: the Philistines have gathered for battle once again, only this time it is not Saul who is against them but David, along with his right-hand man Eleazar, one of these mighty warriors. The story goes that once again 'the people had fled from the Philistines' (v. 13), as they had been doing in the time of Saul (10.1, 7), but now this fellow Eleazar 'and David took their stand in the middle of the plot, defended it, and killed the Philistines' (11.14). So the Philistines are up against a different force now, a force underpinned by Yahweh himself ('and Yahweh saved them by a great victory').

These vignettes demonstrate that no matter how large the enemy forces are now or how mighty they have been in the past, they are no match for David and the people alongside him, his heroes and warriors. Opponents might even carry the title 'Lion of God' (*ari-el* in v. 22 may be a term for a champion with supposedly superhuman strength at his disposal or divine blessing on his exploits, though the NRSV prefers to construe the expression as 'son of Arion'), but they are no match for David's champions, who are also able to overcome actual lions (*ari* later in the same verse) as well. Another opponent is 'an Egyptian, a man of great stature, five cubits tall' (v. 23), something like two meters tall with a very long reach—but not only would the length of such a man's arms give him a considerable advantage, in addition he had at his disposal 'a spear like a weaver's beam'. Such a formidable weapon is also pictured in the hands of another legendary opponent in 20.5, where it is said that David's man Elhanan overcame the Gittite champion Lahmi, 'the shaft of whose spear was like a weaver's beam'. On this occasion David's man is Benaiah (11.22), and his challenger is an unnamed Egyptian (v. 23).

Thus David does not do all the fighting himself, but he has prudently and effectively surrounded himself with a group of hardy fighters, perhaps even a personal 'bodyguard', if the word *mishmaat* in v. 25 is to be so understood. Alternatively, however, that word could be translated as his 'subjects', and thus David is said to have placed Benaiah in a position of authority over the king's subjects. It is a word which presumably denotes people who owe allegiance, or who must obey the king (being a noun from the verb *shama*, 'to hear, obey'). However the word is construed, though, there appears to be a dark underside here: David requires or demands obedience, or does he even require a bodyguard to protect him? Against whom? Against his enemies, such as the Philistines? Or against his own people? It is noticeable in the list of warriors that there are a number of foreigners. Perhaps even more of the names are of foreign origin than is immediately recognizable, but certainly there is at least an Ammonite (v. 39), a Hittite (v. 41), and a Moabite (v. 46) among the warriors loyal to David; it may be too that the Ethrite (v. 40), the Methrite (v. 43), the Tizzite (v. 45), and the Mezabite (v. 47) are also foreigners. It looks like the king has a troop or troops of mercenaries, fighting men who are loyal to him without any clan allegiance within Israel itself and perhaps on that account more ruthless against Israelite opponents as well as against the king's external enemies.

Chapter 12

If it is the case that David has opposition, there is only a hint of it; we have to read between the lines to see it. But the hint that the Annalists want to give us is that David is very much the person whom all Israel wants to see as king. The 'all Israel' drum has been beaten already, but now in ch. 12 further details are given about Israelites coming to support

David. Every tribe is mentioned, including first of all Benjaminites (v. 2), the tribe from whom Saul came—hence the importance of mentioning them first. Although they are 'Saul's kindred', they support David, and in fact they are the first in line to do so. Perhaps they realize that they need quickly to demonstrate support for David or it could be very problematic for them, or more likely the Annalists want us to think that they were for David all along. Next are Gadites (v. 8), then Judahites (v. 16, together with further Benjaminites), Manassites (v. 19), Simeonites (v. 25), Levites (v. 26—even though they are represented as a priestly tribe they are militarily active as well, with thousands of warriors coming forward from that tribe too, together with yet more Benjaminites in v. 29), Ephraimites (v. 30), Issacharites (v. 32), Zebulunites (v. 33), Naphtalites (v. 34), Danites (v. 35), Asherites (v. 36), and Reubenites (v. 37, accompanied by some more Gadites and Manassites). Thus every sub-grouping of Israelites is explicitly named, underpinning by 'facts and figures' that indeed 'all Israel' stands with David (12.38, reiterating 11.1).

Huge numbers of warriors are set out in the Annalists' accounting. The first figure given is 6800 men from Judah (v. 24), followed by 7100 from Simeon (v. 25), then 4600 from Levi (v. 26), and so on. The largest group is from Zebulun, no less than '50,000 seasoned troops' (v. 33) from a tribal group which had not been given a genealogy in the earlier lists but is now most assuredly numbered among the ranked military forces at David's disposal. Similarly Dan had also appeared as though childless among the earlier genealogies but is now equipped with 28,600 soldiers (v. 35). All together, if the figures provided in ch. 12 are added up, there are 339,600 men at arms (plus 1222 'commanders' and 'chiefs' enumerated separately).

Such fantastical numbers are surely given to demonstrate the huge and uncontested nature of David's acclamation as king. Everyone wants to be there to celebrate, and they celebrate in grand style indeed (in vv. 38-40). The coronation feast lasts for three days (another 'three' in this set of stories), with all the assembled multitude eating and drinking their way through the provisions that 'their kindred had provided for them' (v. 39). Thus is depicted a great generosity of spirit on the part of all Israel, a generosity of spirit that will be seen again later in 29.6-9 and yet again in 2 Chron. 30.5-7 and 35.7-9. Perhaps there is a hint of some forced generosity in 1 Chron. 18.2-11 and 20.2, but by and large the Annalists seem at pains to present a picture of unforced generosity, to depict a people only too happy to contribute to events of national rejoicing for all Israel.

'There was joy in Israel' (v. 40). That is what all this elevation of David to the throne is leading to. David is the hero, the saviour of Israel, so naturally there is joy. The same note of joy will come again later (in

15.16, 25; 16.31-33; 29.9; and in 2 Chron. 20.27; 30.26). The Annalists want us to be in no doubt that this is a happy, paradigmatic occasion for Israel. But certain aspects in their account nonetheless sound a somewhat different note, such as the reference to a time at which David 'could not move about freely because of Saul' (12.1). Thus there is a hint that Saul had opposed David or that David had opposed Saul, or that at any rate their relationship was not at ease. There may also be a hint in v. 29, in the reference to 'the majority' of the Benjaminites who 'had continued to keep their allegiance to the house of Saul'. Were there then tribesmen who were not fully in support of David's rise to the throne, and who continued to keep their allegiance to the house of Saul even though the house of Saul had effectively died? Perhaps too v. 17 hints at opposition, not only from Saul's kindred in the tribe of Benjamin but even from David's kindred in the tribe of Judah, for David says to a group of Benjaminites and Judahites who come to his stronghold, 'If you have come to me in friendship, to help me, then my heart will be knit to you; but if you have come to betray me to my adversaries, though my hands have done no wrong, then may the god of our ancestors see and give judgment'.

What is this about adversaries? Nowhere else in this text do we have anybody standing against David, except for the Philistines. But why would Benjaminites and Judahites be coming to betray David into the hands of the Philistines? Could it be because some regard him as being in league with the Philistines? A startling admission is made in v. 19: 'Some of the Manassites deserted to David when he came with the Philistines for the battle against Saul'. So there had been a belief that David was with the Philistines, fighting against Saul—but the Annalists are anxious that we should not believe that, because they say immediately that David did not help the Philistines against Saul. Nonetheless, a few hints have been given that David had some internal opposition, despite that recurring 'all Israel' and 'all the elders of Israel' (11.1-4, 10). Perhaps, after all, 'all' were not for David. He at least appears in 12.17 to express some fears that not all may be with him. And there is also a hint in v. 19's mention of him being 'with the Philistines…against Saul' that there might be some reasons for certain people to be against him. Is that why he needs such huge troops—not just for fighting the Philistines, but to keep his own people on side? And is that why he needs those foreigners in his army—not just as professional soldiers but specifically as non-Israelites beholden to no Israelite but the king?

David's uncertainties expressed in v. 17 about whether there are foes as well as friends within his own tribe are immediately taken care of by a certain individual by the name of Amasai, who steps forward on this singular occasion to enunciate with considerable poetic flair: 'We are yours,

O David, and with you, O son of Jesse! Peace, peace to you, and peace to the one who helps you! For your god is the one who helps you.' It sounds like a battle hymn, and may remind modern readers of the 'for God, king and country' line that has been used in more recent wars. 'We are yours, O David' is the rallying cry for all Israel. With the 'son of Jesse' now enthroned, and the glory days beginning for the fledgling kingdom, the Annalists can speak of 'joy in Israel' (v. 40). David has been elevated to his throne, and everything that these writers hold dear is now possible.

1 Chronicles 13–16:
David's Relocation of his Ark

Chapter 13

The Annalists devote a considerable amount of text to the project of relocating the sacred ark from the outlying town of Kiriath-jearim to the new capital city of Jerusalem. Very little information is provided about this 'ark' as such; readers are presumed to know about so important a cultic object. Its importance in the Annalists' reckoning may be deduced not only from the length of the tale about its progress to Jerusalem, but also from the fact that the project to situate it at Jerusalem is the first activity for which David assembles 'all Israel' (13.5) after he and 'all Israel' had seized control of the city (11.4). Indeed we are perhaps to assume that the project was first mooted very soon after the city was in David's hands, but the narrative flow has been interrupted by the lists of David's warriors and the tribal numbers at the time of the coronation.

More elaboration is given here than had been the case regarding David's very first act as king, namely the takeover of Jerusalem itself. On that occasion it was rather breathlessly reported that 'David and all Israel marched to Jerusalem…and he took the stronghold of Zion, now the city of David' (11.4-5). No consultations were held between David and the assembly as to whether or not such a venture 'seems good to you' or whether 'it is the will of our god Yahweh' (expressions used now in 13.2), no elaborate plans were laid out for how that campaign should be conducted (save for promising the command of the army to whoever took the initiative [11.6]), and no hiccups transpired in the accomplishing of the task (David simply 'took' the city and subsequently 'resided' there [11.5, 7]). But now with the sacred ark, David and his people are seen to spend more time in planning the operation and to experience more difficulty in executing the plan. It is apparently a much simpler affair to take over a well-fortified city than to move a little box from one place to another.

Once again everyone is with David. But the care that he takes, before launching this agenda, to consult with everyone, to see whether there is full agreement that it is a good idea to bring this sacred box from where it is, sets the scene that a very problematic object is being dealt with here. Agreement is reached (v. 4), and the project commences. But just what is this 'ark' (*aron*), variously referred to in this episode as 'the ark of our god' (v. 3), 'the divine ark' (v. 5), 'the ark of Yahweh' (15.3), and 'the ark of the covenant of Yahweh' (15.25), and elsewhere in the Annals also as 'the ark of holiness' (2 Chron. 35.3), or of course simply as 'the ark'? Evidently it is an object believed to have sacredness adhering to it, an object concerning which great care must be taken. Not just anybody can go into sacred places, and not just anybody can handle sacred objects; only certain people can do that, and for others there is grave danger involved. It is evidently associated with Yahweh, and more particularly with the covenant of Yahweh.

A few details of this 'ark' are provided in v. 6, where a somewhat longer expression appears: it is 'the ark of the god Yahweh, who sits upon the cherubs, which is called by his name'. Mysterious creatures known as 'cherubs' appear in certain other ancient Hebrew traditions. In the story of human beginnings, cherubs are appointed to bar the first humans from the primeval garden within which lies the elixir of immortality (Genesis 3.22-24); accordingly it may be deduced that in the Hebrew imagination cherubs are associated with protecting places that the divine will intends to keep from human disposition. Having cherubs associated with this box works well in that context, as well as suggesting a connection with the Annalists' interest (to be seen in ch. 26) in gatekeepers for the sacred precincts, charged with the duty of keeping the profane away from the holy. Cherubs also make appearances in the hymnic traditions of Israel. For example, Psalm 18.10, in singing of the awesome activities of Yahweh, includes the following dramatic image: 'He rode on a cherub, and flew; he came swiftly upon the wings of the wind'. Psalm 99.1 proclaims: 'Yahweh is king; let the peoples tremble! He sits upon the cherubs; let the earth quake!' Such imagery suggests that the heavenly king sits enthroned upon cherubs, and perhaps that the Annalists might think of the 'ark' as a representation of Yahweh's throne, or at least a symbol of his presence among his people.

If this ark is a symbol of divine kingship, then it is very significant to be associated with David, whom the Annalists are establishing as king on Yahweh's behalf. In 14.2 they say that 'David perceived that Yahweh had established him as king over Israel, and that his kingdom was highly exalted for the sake of his people Israel'. Is it David's kingdom or is it Yahweh's kingdom? Is it David's people Israel or is it Yahweh's people Israel? Or are they one and the same thing? As often in Hebrew, the pronoun has some slippage about it. But it is evident that this ark which symbolizes Yahweh's reigning in the heavens ought to be with David, who wants to be reigning in Yahweh's kingdom on earth. In 16.31, in the psalm that is sung when David finally brings the ark into Jerusalem, there is a reference to Yahweh's kingship; but of course it is King David who wants to prove his own regal legitimacy as well. An interesting reference is in 2 Chron. 13.8, where David's great-grandson Abijah addresses the army of the northern kingdom which has broken away from the Davidic monarchy: 'You think you can withstand the kingdom of Yahweh in the hands of the sons of David!' It is a powerful royal ideology: the throne in Jerusalem is the seat of the kingdom of Yahweh in the hands of the sons of David. So David reigns for Yahweh; accordingly he must have this symbol of Yahweh's rule with him in Jerusalem.

The Annals provide some details about what is in the ark, telling us indeed that 'there was nothing in the ark except the two tablets that Moses put there at Horeb' (2 Chron. 5.10) and speaking of 'the ark, in which is the covenant of Yahweh that he made with the people of Israel' (2 Chron. 6.11). The Annalists may expect that their readers know something of the traditions concerning the ark that have come down to us in such biblical passages as Exodus 25.10-22, which describes 'an ark of acacia wood...two and a half cubits long, a cubit and a half wide, and a cubit and a half high', overlaid 'with pure gold, inside and outside', and 'a moulding of gold upon it all round'; but they may prefer their readers to be unfamiliar with such details, and rather to imagine something of even grander dimensions—after all, they tell us that 'the poles [by which the ark was carried] were so long that [when the sacred box was placed in the temple] the ends of the poles were seen from the holy place in front of the inner sanctuary' (2 Chron. 5.9). (Incidentally, the English word 'ark' is used in biblical translations also for the huge boat that Noah used to save himself and his human and animal companions from the great flood, but in fact in Hebrew these are two different words, so the Annalists are not thinking in Noahic proportions for this more modest vessel.)

An important thing to notice in the introduction to the episode of David and the ark is that we are seeing a contrast between those who went before David and the regime of David himself. David says (in 13.3), 'Let us bring the ark of our god to us, for we did not seek it in the days of Saul'. Readers will recall that precisely that was the problem with Saul, as expressed in 10.14: he did not seek Yahweh, but sought other things. This will be the basis on which all the later kings are judged by the Annalists: whether or not they seek Yahweh. Saul's error lay in his failure to do so, as represented by an implied neglect of this sacred object. David seeks to rectify this Israelite failure.

And where is this 'ark' at the moment? In the town of Kiriath-jearim (v. 5), alternatively designated as Baalah and situated within the tribal territory of Judah (v. 6). Is it there because Saul did not care about it? Saul was a Benjaminite, but it may have been of no consequence to him which territory the ark lay in. Or could it be there in the hands of one of

Saul's people? We are told that the ark is taken 'from the house of Abinadab' (v. 7). Now that is a name that intriguingly occurs in two of the earlier genealogies: one of Saul's sons is called Abinadab (8.33; 9.39), but his death is also referred to (10.2); and one of David's brothers is similarly called Abinadab (2.13). Are the Annalists wanting us to think that this Abinadab living in Kiriath-jearim is one of those two people? If so, why do they not tell us which one? Does David's brother have it for safekeeping? Or is it after all in the house of Saul, who has not looked after it properly or did not 'seek it' and therefore it needs to be taken away? These are intriguing interpretive possibilities, but the lack of details suggest that the Annalists want us to think that it is another Abinadab entirely, that it is of no consequence who that Abinadab is. The important thing is that it is not where it ought to be, in its own house, but is in the house of somebody else.

In due course the ark moves from the house of Abinadab, but only as far as 'the house of Obed-edom the Gittite' (13.13). This too is an intriguing detail not fleshed out by the Annalists, leaving readers to speculate. Why the house of a Gittite—that is, a person from the Philistine city of Gath? And moreover someone with the name Obed-edom—that is, 'slave of Edom'! However, despite its less than auspicious meaning, Obed-edom is a name that occurs a number of times in the earlier Israelite genealogies. Is this man, then, an Israelite who lives (or used to live) in a Philistine city (or a former Philistine city), or is he actually a Philistine? Could David be leaving the ark with the Philistines because it is too dangerous to be with the Israelites? That would seem rather bizarre, since the whole reason for moving the ark is to have it with the king of Israel in Jerusalem, to place it under his care and at his disposal in the royal centre. Is Obed-edom somebody expendable—such that it does not matter if his life is in danger through having this highly dangerous object in his possession—or is he somebody dependable—such that he will make sure that it is attended properly?

Could he perhaps be a Levite, given that the name 'Obed-edom' comes up quite frequently in the levitical lists? The several occurrences of that name among the Levites (15.18, 21, 24, 25; 16.5, 38; 26.4-8) presumably designate many different Obed-edoms and so indicate a certain popularity of the name in levitical circles (or a certain lack of imagination among the Annalists in plotting levitical ancestors). Accordingly a reader may be forgiven for contemplating the possibility that the Annalists think of this Obed-edom as being a Levite too, although calling him a Gittite (v. 13) might dampen such speculation somewhat. Nevertheless, it is noteworthy that the Obed-edom mentioned in 15.24 is one of two 'gatekeepers for the ark'. If there is a Levite of that name who is a gatekeeper of the ark once it is in Jerusalem, it is possible that we are supposed to think of him here as the keeper of the ark before it comes to Jerusalem, particularly since the reference to the so-named individual being a gatekeeper (in 15.24) is followed immediately by the account of 'David and the elders of Israel and the commanders of the thousands [going] to bring up the ark of the covenant from the house of Obed-edom with rejoicing' (15.25). Is this meant to be the same person, or is it a coincidence?

But why does David not take the ark to Jerusalem straight away? Well, an interesting incident intervenes during the journey 'when they came to the threshing-floor of Chidon' (13.9): a man by the name of Uzzah, one of two men who had been charged with the responsibility of driving the oxen-powered cart on which the ark was being carried (v. 7), put out his hand to steady the ark when 'the oxen shook it' (v. 9). Presumably the precious cargo was in danger of sliding off the cart on account of the condition of the path or the excitability of the oxen, but the unfortunate Uzzah dies during the incident. The way the Annalists record matters is that 'Yahweh's anger was kindled against Uzzah, and he struck him down because he had put out his hand to the ark' (v. 10). Uzzah dies there on the spot as a direct and immediate punishment for the offence against the deity of touching the sacred box. Later the king will comment that only Levites should handle the ark, and even then poles should be used to avoid touching the box itself (15.11-15). Thus the storytellers associate phenomenal magic with this ark, and all who read or hear the story might well be motivated to entrust the care and functioning of sacred matters to the Levites alone.

It is interesting that this happens at a threshing-floor, since the site where the ark will be placed permanently, the site where the temple in Jerusalem will be built, is also a threshing-floor (21.18; 22.1). We might wonder what it is about threshing-floors that lead to their appearances with significance in these ancient Annals. In this particular episode, why is the ark shaken when it comes to a threshing-floor? The Annalists may have in mind a purely random shaking which might have happened any-where, and thus we ought to view it as a matter of coincidence that they picture the event as happening at a threshing-floor, but it is a curious detail that it is said to have happened just at such a place. Threshing-floors are of course places where grain is threshed as part of the harvest process; that is, pieces of grain are shaken from the stalks on which they were grown. The wheat is separated from the chaff. As a place of separa-tion, the imagery of a place for divine judgment may come to mind. Given the central importance of the harvest (and given—though the Annalists would probably not want us to think too strongly in this direction—the heritage of earlier fertility-religion), these were presumably places where people made prayers and sacrifices in order that the fertility of the land might be ensured through the fertility of the seeds being harvested. So too threshing-floors may be located on the tops of hills to take advantage of a good wind, and since hilltops and high places were associated with religious practice in the early days, so there may be some analogy to such matters at work in this story.

Whatever the background for weaving this particular tale, the chosen expression is that 'Yahweh's anger was kindled' (v. 10)—literally, 'Yahweh's nose became hot', a Hebrew idiom somewhat akin to the English phrase 'he got hot under the collar'. In turn David too 'was angry' (v. 11), although in his case matters are expressed less graphically by the shorter expression 'he became hot', with no reference to his nose as such. It is interesting that such an idiom is used for the deity, that Yahweh is in a way pictured as having a nose that can show its red coloration when he is angry at somebody touching his magic box, but for David, who literally has a nose, the same expression is not used.

The place-name Perez-uzzah is presumably a very famous one. In the genealogies the Annalists sometimes included details about how certain people got their names or how certain places got theirs, and now here they do the same. Yahweh had 'burst out against' or 'perezed' (the verb is employed here in the form *paratz*) the unfortunate man, so 'The Perezing of Uzzah' or 'Uzzah's Rupture' commemorates the incident. 'Uzzah' itself denotes 'strength', and indeed one of the names for the ark is 'the ark of your [i.e. Yahweh's] strength' (*aron uzzecha*, 2 Chron. 6.41). But this strong man Uzzah is no match for the strength of Yahweh when the deity is angered by some untoward activity like this.

Note the difference between what happens to Uzzah and what happens to Obed-edom. There is no divine anger toward the house of Obed-edom, but rather blessing. That means either that Obed-edom was a Levite or that he treated the ark with sufficient respect—nobody touched it or nobody went into the tent where he kept it. And notice too that in ch. 13 the ark is taken from one house to another house and then at the beginning of ch. 14 David sets about building a house for himself; any plan to create a house for the ark in Jerusalem has been put on hold. The king has been left unsure about his project of bringing the ark to Jerusalem, and it will be some time before he resolves upon a more successful strategy regarding its transportation (at the beginning of ch. 15).

Chapter 14

In addition to 'building a house' for himself with the assistance of the neighbouring king of Tyre (14.1), the new king of Israel also 'took more wives in Jerusalem' (v. 3). Whatever we moderns think of that sort of activity, as full ruler now he can do it. In the genealogies in ch. 3 David's wives were named, but here in the narrative they are not. One of the daughters was also named in ch. 3, but here, although it is stated that 'David became the father of more sons and daughters, and these are the names of the children' (vv. 3-4), in fact only the names of the sons are presented—and indeed with some different names in certain cases than those that were listed in ch. 3. It makes more sense that in the list of names that are presented here (in 14.4-7) we have 'Elishua and Elpelet' instead of 'Elishama and Eliphelet', because the names 'Elishama' and 'Eliphelet' occur later in the list. Nonetheless such discrepancies between the two lists make it appear that the Annalists cannot get their story entirely straight—or perhaps we should rather say that the scribes responsible for transmitting the text of the Annals have not been able to get all the names entirely right.

After the listing of David's Jerusalemite sons, we are told (in 14.8) that the Philistines plan to do to David exactly what they had done to Saul. The same Hebrew verb is used here as had been employed in 10.8, and it resonates with the name of the raiders themselves: there 'the Philistines' (*plishtim*) 'stripped' (*pashat*) the dead; here 'the Philistines' (*plishtim*) 'made a raid' (*pashat*) in the valley of Rephaim. Perhaps the Philistines are so called because they are raiders and plunderers, or at least the Annalists think that a suggestive play-on-words can be made. They are up to the same thing again in 14.13, so this seems to be the only activity that they can do. But on these occasions they will not be successful, for now they are dealing with David, a man who seeks divine counsel, the very thing that his predecessor Saul had not done. David 'asks' (*sha'al*, vv. 10, 13) the deity whether he should launch an attack against the raiders; Saul (*sha'ul*, the one supposedly 'asked for') had in fact 'asked' (*sha'al*, 10.13) a medium.

We are not told precisely how David puts his question to the heavens nor how the divine response is communicated. The text rather matter-of-factly has it that 'David inquired of the deity…and Yahweh said to him…' (v. 10), 'and again David inquired of the deity, and the deity said to him…' (v. 14). We might speculate how the Annalists imagine this was done. Did David throw Urim and Thummim, those oracular devices mentioned in other ancient Hebrew traditions as ways in which the priests can perceive the divine will (e.g. Exodus 28.30; Ezra 2.63)? Does David ask a priest directly for an oracle, and the priest goes into a trance or opens up a bird to study its entrails and thus decides that the omens are favourable? Perhaps there is some other way that David can decide whether the omens are favourable or not. Perhaps the Annalists want us to think that David and Yahweh speak face to face; after all, other Hebrew storytellers told of such figures as Abraham or Moses conversing with Yahweh and even conducting quite elaborate conversations with him (e.g. Genesis 15; Exodus 3). The first divine message here (in v. 10) is not particularly elaborate, but the second one received (in vv. 14-15) is somewhat more so. Accordingly, perhaps we are meant to think that David has a special hotline to heaven, that he speaks directly to his god. And his god assures him, by whatever means the king believes—or the storytellers believe—the deity to convey such matters, that 'I will give them [i.e. the Philistines] into your hands'. This development contrasts with the fate of the previous regime: Yahweh had not delivered the Philistines into Saul's hands, but instead had delivered Saul into the hands of the Philistines. David will be crowned with success, and his first dramatic victory against the Philistines is enshrined in the battle-site's name, Baal-perazim (v. 11: *ba'al peratzim* means 'Lord of Burstings'), related to the victorious monarch's cry, 'the deity has burst out (*paratz*) against my enemies…like the bursting out (*peretz*) of waters'. Readers will recall the earlier association of divine 'bursting out' against Uzzah with the place-name Perez-uzzah (13.11), but the present unleashing of divine power works to the advantage of the king and his people.

In v. 16 'David did as the deity had commanded him'—again unlike Saul, who did not follow the divine plans as David now does. The key to success throughout these Annals is: do what the deity commands you, and all will be well. The divine instructions given here are actually to wait for the deity himself to do the business; Yahweh will cause a noise 'in the tops of the balsam trees' to make the Philistines think that a great and in fact heavenly army is upon them. One might call to mind the expression 'Yahweh of hosts' or 'Yahweh of armies' (an expression used in 11.9 and 17.7, 24): the deity is perceived in certain respects as a military figure, and he will fight for David.

Chapter 15

Having had success against the Philistines, David makes a new attempt to bring the ark to Jerusalem. Could it be that he was not able to succeed in bringing the ark to Jerusalem partly because the Philistine threat had not been settled? Obed-edom being a 'Gittite' could be a hint that the Philistines had some control over the ark for a time. In any event David now seems to realize somehow what he had done wrong in his initial attempt to relocate the ark to Jerusalem. He must use the Levites: 'Then David commanded that no one but the Levites were to carry the sacred ark, for Yahweh had chosen them to carry the ark of Yahweh and to minister to him forever' (15.2). This is reiterated in v. 15: 'and the Levites carried the sacred ark on their shoulders with the poles, as Moses had commanded according to the word of Yahweh'. (This is indeed in accordance with the traditions recorded in Exodus 25.14, Numbers 1.50-51 and Deuteronomy 31.25.) We are not told why David knows about this now whereas he had not known about it earlier, but now that he has issued such instructions, all should be well.

According to the figures in vv. 5-10, he has assembled no less than 862 Levites with him to bring the ark to Jerusalem, whereas on the first abortive attempt he had had a mere two men working on the case, Uzzah and Ahio (13.7), though with 'all Israel dancing before the deity with all their might, with song and lyres and harps and tambourines and cymbals and trumpets' (13.8). On this second occasion he has organized things more systematically, it seems, and has put together a better-organized procession with the right functionaries in place: over 800 people in procession and lots of musical accompaniment to go with it, for this time David has commanded that Levites be appointed 'as the singers to play on musical instruments, on harps and lyres and cymbals' (15.16). The Annalists are pleased to list names of the properly appointed levitical cymbalists (v. 19), harpists (v. 20), lyrists (v. 21), and trumpeters (v. 24) as a means of fleshing out the scene of a grand procession befitting the movement of this very significant ark.

So too they provide us with details that we do not know much about: that the harps were to be played 'according to *alamoth*' (v. 20) and that the lyres were to be played 'according to the *sheminith*' (v. 21). These are obscure words that also occur in one or two places in the book of Psalms: the superscription to Psalm 46 includes the note 'according to *alamoth*', which appears to be an instruction about how you are to play that particular song; and the superscriptions to Psalms 6 and 12 include the words 'according to the *sheminith*'. Nothing is said either in those psalms or here in these Annals as to what these terms mean as such. Are they styles of music or particular tunes that are meant to be played? *Alamoth* literally means 'young women' or 'girls', so was there a famous song about young women, a tune that you were supposed to play here? Presumably it is not that young women are supposed to play this, as the Annalists are picturing an all-male procession of singers and instrumentalists. No women are seen as being permitted to go anywhere near the ark. *Sheminith*, on the other hand, means 'eighth', so was there a 'Song (or Tune) Number Eight' in the levitical repertoire? But while we do not understand what these things are, v. 22 says that 'Chenaniah, leader of the Levites in music, was to direct the music, for he understood it' (if indeed it is music that is indicated there, as the Hebrew word *massa* could be translated as the 'carrying' of the ark and so the whole procession may be what is being referred to as the matter that Chenaniah understood, directing the entire event rather than simply the 'music'). In any event, whatever the particular details of *alamoth* and *sheminith* refer to, the people involved in the procession are certainly doing it all 'with rejoicing' (v. 25), according to the Annalists, who evidently have a liking for depicting these grand occasions of Israelite assembly as exceedingly joyful occasions (cf. 1 Chron. 12.40; 29.9; 2 Chron. 7.10; 30.26).

However, there is an intriguing note at the end of the chapter, in v. 29, that as the ark came into the city of David, Michal the daughter of Saul saw it and was not impressed: 'she despised him [i.e. King David] in her heart'. This is the only mention of a female member of the house of Saul in the Annals. We are not told anything else about her, just that she is Saul's daughter, that she is in David's city, and that she despises David, possibly as a result of seeing him 'leaping and dancing'. Is it that she feels that her father should be the rightful king and not this David, with whose name the city is now associated ('the city of David')? What is she doing in what is now David's city if she was from Saul's household? None of that is told to us, but again it is an interesting note that the Annalists let slip that in fact not all of Israel is rejoicing, not everyone is with David in everything that he does.

Chapter 16

The sacred ark is now 'brought in' to the city and 'set inside the tent that David had pitched for it' (16.1), whereupon various kinds of offerings are made to the deity. The activities here have the hallmarks of a ceremony of institution for a permanent home for the ark, although there is not yet a house—that is still to come. David seems to be doing the offering, or at least instigating it, and he does the blessing in v. 2. These are things that one presumes the priests should be doing. Indeed there is a rather interesting story in 2 Chron. 26.18, when a king tries to do what the priests should be doing in terms of making offerings, and he suffers as a result, being struck down with leprosy because of this crime. Such a punishment is perhaps not as bad as what happened to Uzzah for touching the ark, but it is still bad news. Yet here David does the same with impunity. Thus this foundational monarch is somebody precious; although he is not a priest or a Levite, he alone (apart from his immediate successor Solomon) is permitted by the Annalists to do priestly things that they normally reserve for the priestly classes.

A long song is sung in vv. 8-36, a hymn which has echoes from other songs to be found in the book of Psalms. Note that in v. 7 the song is introduced by saying that it was 'on that day', the day that David had bought the ark to Jerusalem, that 'David first appointed the giving of thanks to Yahweh by Asaph and his kindred', by these particular Levites with a specialism in singing. The phrase 'the giving of thanks' (*hodoth*) links with the first words of the psalm here, 'O give thanks (*hodu*) to Yahweh' (v. 8), but the NRSV translators prefer to speak more generally of 'the singing of praises' rather than specifically of thanksgiving. The important thing for the Annalists is that the giving of thanks or the singing of praises predates the temple itself and is instituted by David, and is not an innovation devised, say, during the reign of King Hezekiah or Josiah, as good as those monarchs are, and certainly not a post-exilic innovation. No, it is instituted by David himself. Indeed it is not said to have been instituted by Aaron or by Moses; these customs do not predate David, apparently. The Annalists are not making a claim that everything began with Moses; in fact they do not mention Moses a great deal, other than to say that David is doing things in a particular way which is in accordance with the word of Yahweh as given by Moses. But it seems that for the Annalists David is much more important than Moses. They very much want to ground these things in the time of David, as the time of the founding of Israelite national life.

After the psalm is over David leaves the people he has appointed to those tasks 'to minister regularly before the ark' (v. 37). He also leaves 'the priest Zadok and his kindred the priests before the tabernacle of Yahweh in the high place that was at Gibeon' (v. 39). So for the moment there will be a high place, a kind of temple where the priests will be consultable, outside of Jerusalem in Gibeon, the place tainted with Saul's failure. This will not do long-term; David will have to do something about it, and indeed immediately in the next chapter he will be thinking to do something about it. Not doing anything about it now arguably goes against the things that are 'written in the laws of Yahweh that he commanded Israel', even though v. 40 is at pains to say that offering these offerings every morning and evening is 'according to all that is written in the law of Yahweh that he commanded Israel', for if one consults Exodus 40.5, 21 (which the Annalists may not wish their readers to do on the matter), one sees that the ark of the covenant is meant to be at the place where these morning and evening sacrifices are being made. Thus David could be seen as not doing 'all' precisely right at this stage. Nonetheless, seeing to it that offerings are made every morning and evening is certainly in accord with the traditions represented in Exodus 29.38-41 and Numbers 28.3-4.

Apart from that little detail (which the story will see to immediately in the next chapter) of not having a permanent and proper house for the ark and not having the priests doing the offerings in the same place as the ark, everything is accomplished—at least insofar as David has now brought the ark to Jerusalem and it will never leave there again (that is to say, the Annals do not speak of it ever leaving Jerusalem). For the moment the ark has no permanent home, while 'all the people departed to their homes, and David went to bless his home' (or NRSV 'household' [v. 43]). Each family has its own house; the deity will have to have one as well. This little symbolic throne or footstool by itself will not be enough for the god of Israel. David at this time blesses his house, but there is a bigger blessing to come from Yahweh upon the house of David. Nevertheless, for the moment there is quite a sense of accomplishment here: when the episode of ark-relocation began back in ch. 13 the sacred box was in the house of an obscure person, but now at the ending of the episode it is firmly ensconced in the city of David.

1 Chronicles 17:
David's Estimation of his Reign

King David is now 'settled in his house' (17.1), and can sit back to contemplate his achievements and aspirations. The simple word 'house' has
already figured prominently in the Annalists' account, with a great deal of
scene-setting about houses in the narrative leading up to this point—not
only has the king 'built houses for himself in the city of David' (15.1), but
the sacred ark has been successively moved 'from the house of Abinadab'
(13.7) and 'from the house of Obed-edom' (15.25) to the same city of
David, with the result that 'all the people' are able to return happily 'to
their houses' and the king is able 'to bless his house' (16.43)—and now
the word will appear no less than 14 times in ch. 17.

   David is 'living in a house of cedar, but the ark of the covenant of
Yahweh is under a tent' (17.1), so the implications of what had been pictured back at the beginning of ch. 15 are now drawn out. In 15.1 we
were told that David 'built houses for himself in the city of David'—not
just one house but 'houses' in the plural. The king has a large family who
cannot readily fit under one roof, no matter how large the building (the
genealogy of David in 3.1-9 had listed seven wives and implied that there
were more, and had named 19 sons and a daughter while leaving the
children of the secondary wives unnamed and unnumbered; then the
account of David's exploits had reiterated in 14.3-7 that his family grew
by at least 13 sons during his Jerusalem years). He is probably also providing accommodation within the court for various retainers and courti-
ers. But in any case he has his own personal dwelling, 'a house of cedar',
built before he raises any plan for building a similar dwelling for Yahweh,
for whom he has until now merely 'pitched a tent' (15.1). A commensu-
rate 'house' for his god was not the monarch's first thought. Nonetheless,
since David's first thought after his coronation was to conquer Jerusalem
and then his second thought was to try to move the sacred ark to that
city, it is a natural development in these Annals that he should now
realize that he ought to be doing something about where his god is living,
now that the king himself is living in a fine house within his 'city of
David'.

   As in the case of the ark-moving project, on which the king first consults with the people concerning what he had in mind (13.1-4), David
does not proceed without speaking to somebody about his plans. This
time he speaks to just one person, to the prophet Nathan (17.1), whose
first and only active appearance in the Annals is in this particular

episode. The name 'Nathan' appears elsewhere, however. Actually in the list of David's sons in 3.5 and again in 14.4, the two places where the sons of David who are born in Jerusalem are mentioned, there is a 'Nathan' among them, but it is unlikely that the Annalists want us to think that the prophet appearing on the scene at this stage is the son of David. The only son of David that readers are meant to think of as having any significant role is the future king Solomon (although he is not mentioned by name in this episode, there are several references to a particular 'son of David' and in the unfolding narrative that is evidently Solomon). There are three later references in the Annals to a prophet Nathan having been active in David's time: in 29.29, where David has died and a formulaic expression concerning such-and-such contemporaneous prophets is used, with Nathan being one of three so listed; in 2 Chron. 9.29, where Solomon has died and the same way of speaking about the lifetime of a king is employed, with Nathan being mentioned alongside two further prophets; and finally in 2 Chron. 29.25, where we find the expression 'according to the commandment of David and of Gad the king's seer and of the prophet Nathan, for the commandment was from Yahweh through his prophets'.

Thus there are some allusions to Nathan later on, as well as to another prophet or seer who worked at the time of David, namely Gad (who will appear in the episode of selecting the site for the house of Yahweh in ch. 21). But the only narrative in the Annals in which we find Nathan interacting with David is the present episode. Since 'Nathan' is a name that David gave to one of his sons born in Jerusalem, as well as being the name of the prophet who appears on the scene now that David has settled in the city, it may be that he is a Jerusalemite himself, perhaps one who functioned as a prophet in the city already before David conquered it. There is after all a possible hint in the genealogies (in 8.28, 32, although it looks suspiciously like a mistake over against the post-exilic listings in 9.34, 38) that Benjaminites were living in the city of Jebus/Jerusalem, perhaps alongside non-Israelite Jebusites, before David made it his very own city.

Here we have an account of David needing to seek the authority of a prophet, whereas earlier on there had been seemingly direct words between David and Yahweh. Readers will recall in ch. 14 that David simply speaks directly to Yahweh and Yahweh directly answers him, at least on a literal reading: 'David asked the deity, "Shall I go up against the Philistines? Will you give them into my hand?", and Yahweh said to him, "Go up, and I will give them into your hand"' (14.10). Very similar expressions appear in v. 14 as well, with David again making an inquiry and receiving a direct divine response, on that occasion a longer piece of advice. Perhaps the Annalists do not really want us to think of the king and his god speaking face to face, but the way in which they tell the story suggests such a picture. On this later occasion, though, David seeks a word of assurance from an intermediary rather than speaking directly to the heavens.

The prophet's initial response is favourable, but after he has slept on it he takes a somewhat different view. 'That same night the word of Yahweh came to him' (17.3), and then 'in accordance with all these words and all this vision, Nathan spoke to David' (v. 15). It seems that David himself does not have visions, but his prophet does, and the vision says that what David has in mind is not exactly to be followed through. This is despite the prophet having at first said, in effect, 'Yes, do it, because the deity is with you' (v. 2), and the Annalists do want us to think that indeed his god is with David in virtually everything that he does. There is hardly a chapter in the David section of the Annals that does not make that clear in one way or another. If we look for example at 11.2, we see the people of Israel saying to David in Hebron, 'Your god Yahweh said to you, "It is you who shall be shepherd of my people Israel, you who shall be ruler over my people Israel"'. And in 12.18 one particular man of Israel, Amasai, chief of the Thirty, has a divine spirit come upon him and he says, among other things, 'Your god is the one who helps you'. This confident thread is unravelled slightly in 13.12, where David is afraid of Yahweh because of the divine bursting-out against Uzzah, which makes it appear that David's god is not entirely 'with' him in that first attempt to move the ark to Jerusalem. But then in 14.17 we are told that 'the fame of David went out into all lands, and Yahweh brought the fear of him on all nations', a statement that comes after the narrative of Yahweh helping David, being 'with' him in various battles. In ch. 15, the second attempt to bring the ark to Jerusalem, the implication is very much that Yahweh is with him because he has done the right preparation and has made sure that the right people are carrying the ark. In 16.1 the ark is placed 'inside the tent that David had pitched for it, and they offered burnt-offerings and offerings of well-being before the deity'. So everything is well: Yahweh is with David, and indeed Yahweh himself confirms that now in 17.8: 'I have been with you wherever you went'. So in terms of the narrative in the Annals, Nathan was quite right to have said 'the deity is with you' (v. 2), but it turns out he was wrong to have implied that David should build the temple he had 'in mind'. David had not said in so many words that he was thinking to build a house for Yahweh, but that is the clear implication of what he said in v. 1.

The implications of the divine message beginning in v. 4 are not entirely clear. It could be read as saying that no one is to build Yahweh a house, or as saying that David is not the one who is to build that house. In the Hebrew it is perhaps a little clearer, given the appearance of the personal pronoun, which need not have been included unless emphasis was intended: '*You* shall not build me a house'. It comes as a bit of a surprise in the narrative that Yahweh does not immediately approve David's plan—although we must remember that Yahweh did not immediately enable David to bring the ark into the city, so that may indicate some divine resistance to having or living in a house. And that is how vv. 5-6 seem to read, that Yahweh has never lived in a house and has never commanded any of the leaders of Israel to construct a house for him. He seems to be quite happy with the idea of being a more mobile god, moving around with the people as they moved around. But later on (in v. 9) the speech indicates that the people will no longer be moving around, and therefore by implication it is appropriate that Yahweh too no longer needs to be moving around. Nonetheless it is interesting that in the 12 verses given to this oracle, eight verses talk about not building a house for Yahweh (vv. 4-11)—'No, no, don't build me a house, I've never asked for a house'—and only three verses actually talk about building one (vv. 12-14)—'OK, let it be built, but don't you build it, David'.

The reason for David not building the house is not given as a personal one here; it is not said that 'You are ineligible to be the temple builder because of this reason or that reason', although such will be said later. In 22.7-8, when David is speaking to Solomon about why he had not built the house for Yahweh, he says, 'My son, I had planned to build a house to the name of my god Yahweh, but the word of Yahweh came to me, saying, "You have shed much blood and have waged great wars; you shall not build a house to my name, because you have shed so much blood in my sight on the earth"'. But what the king reports to his son and successor in ch. 22 as the heavenly communication is not divulged to the reader in ch. 17; rather that Yahweh has not had need of a house or has not desired to live in one. In 2 Chron. 6.4-9, when Solomon speaks on the occasion of bringing the ark into the temple that he has now built, and he refers to why it is that his father had not built the temple, he says at some length: 'Blessed be Yahweh, the god of Israel, who with his hand has fulfilled what he promised with his mouth to my father David saying, "Since the day that I brought my people out of the land of Egypt, I have not chosen a city from any of the tribes of Israel in which to build a house, so that my name might be there, and I chose no one as ruler over my people Israel, but I have chosen Jerusalem in order that my name may be there, and I have chosen David to be over my people Israel". My father David had it in mind to build a house for the name of Yahweh, the god of Israel, but Yahweh said to my father David, "You did well to consider building a house for my name; nevertheless, you shall not build the house, but your son that shall be born to you shall build the house for my name."' That is yet another somewhat divergent account of the divine message to David. It is more non-committal there, with no particular reason given for why the founding monarch will not build the temple, none of the 'blood on his hands' idea that 22.8 speaks of. Here in ch. 17 too, there is no explicit message of an ineligibility for temple-building on David's part. What appears in the oracle is a kind of theo-logical resistance to pinning the deity down, but an acceptance of it insofar as the people are now going to be in one place, this being part of the divine plan that David subdue all the enemies of Israel (as v. 9 puts it, Yahweh is going to 'plant' Israel, 'so that they may live in their own place and be disturbed no more').

Notice the reference in two places within this divine speech to the 'judges' of Israel (in v. 6 and again in v. 10). This is the only mention in the Annals of pre-monarchic leaders. We had the brief story of Saul's demise as king, but no stories are told about any previous way in which the tribes of Israel might have been organized, no account of figures called 'judges' as having been active as dispensers of governance and jus-tice. Certainly no details are given here, but an idea presented a little earlier (in 11.2) is recalled, namely the idea of shepherding the people: these judges were 'commanded to shepherd my people' (v. 6), and David is addressed with the words 'I took you from the pasture, from following the sheep' (v. 7). Perhaps this is meant to be a biographical detail about David, that before he became a king he had been a shepherd in the more literal sense, or it may be just a metaphor of the kingly destiny that he had—that is to say, the Annalists may picture David as a shepherd simply because the nation's leader is a metaphorical shepherd. 2 Chronicles 18.16 uses this kind of metaphor, when the prophet Micaiah says, 'I saw all Israel scattered on the mountains, like sheep without a shepherd, and Yahweh said, "These have no master; let each one go home in peace"'. Reading something of that imagery back here, the prophetic message is that Israel needs David as its shepherd in order that a new and better situation can be created. Other people had previously been commanded to shepherd Israel, v. 6 says, but vv. 9-10 make it clear that evil-doers were wearing Israel down when those 'judges' were doing the shepherding; 'judges' had not been a good enough system. Thus even though Yahweh might have been willing to move about with the Israelites ('wherever I have moved about', v. 6), he also presumably wants the situation to change so that he does not have to move about anymore.

Then in v. 8, the words 'I have been with you wherever you went' imply that David also has been moving about; that period is similarly at an end now. What is more, 'I will make for you a name, like the name of the great ones of the earth' (v. 8). In fact in these Annals David's name is greater than any of 'the great ones of the earth'. The Annalists tell no stories about pharaohs or mighty emperors, except tangentially as they interact with the Davidic kings (such as Neco of Egypt defeating Josiah at Megiddo in 2 Chron. 35.20-24) or enable possibilities for Israel (such as Cyrus of Persia mandating the rebuilding of Jerusalem in 2 Chron. 36.22-23). Thus David has an unparalleled name in these Annals; if anyone approaches him, it is his son Solomon who comes after him and who is also referred to (by implication) in this oracle. It is interesting, then, that in his response to the oracle this unparalleled monarch does not say, 'Oh, how wonderful that you are making a name for me!' (although he does say, 'Oh, how wonderful that you are doing this thing for my house!'), but instead he speaks of Yahweh's name: 'making for yourself a name for great and terrible things' (v. 21); 'thus your name will be established and magnified forever in the saying, "Yahweh of hosts, the god of Israel, is Israel's god"' (v. 24). The royal words link that with 'the house of your servant David' (also v. 24), but there is no response as such to the divine message that the deity will make a name for the king.

Another noteworthy matter in the prophetic oracle is v. 8's pronouncement, 'I have cut off all your enemies before you'. The action has been completed, evidently referring back to the various incidents that were presented in chs. 11 and 14, where David was effective against the Jebusites and various Philistines and others. But then v. 10 promises, 'I will subdue all your enemies'. So it is not completed after all; there are more enemies yet to be cut off before David, in stories that will be presented in chs. 18, 19, and 20. There is something of a discrepancy between 'I have cut off all your enemies' in v. 8 and 'I will subdue all your enemies' in v. 10, but the two perspectives make a certain sense within the presentation of David's career.

Yahweh says 'No' to David's plan to build him a house, but in v. 10 the deity turns the tables and says that he will build a house for the king. This is almost a pun, with the word 'house' in Hebrew (*bayit*) having a considerable referential range. Obviously in this latter case it means that Yahweh will create a dynasty for David, that the new monarch's family line or royal house will be firmly established, as no other house in Israel had been (none of the 'judges', and certainly not Saul, had had their house built by Yahweh, but David's house will be so built). The other evident sense of 'house' in this episode is of course the home or temple of a god, and that house is not to be built just yet, but 'when your days are fulfilled to go to be with your ancestors, I will raise up your offspring after you, one of your own sons, and I will establish his kingdom; he shall build a house for me, and I will establish his throne forever' (vv. 11-12). The oracle does not name the chosen one from among the king's sons, and in 14.4-6 readers had been given a long list of regal sons. But there is no real dramatic suspense here—which son will it be?—because we know from the earlier list in 3.5-10, given that the genealogy of Solomon was pictured continuing on down the succeeding generations whereas lines of descent from the other sons were not presented, that it will be Solomon. Nevertheless, the Annalists prefer not to make any explicit naming of Solomon in the oracle itself (though they will have David tell it more explicitly in 22.9).

There are further plays on the words 'father' and 'son' in this oracle: 'I will be a father to him, and he shall be a son to me' (v. 13). The concept of divine adoption of the king—the new monarch at his coronation being formally adopted as the offspring of the national god—is to be found within the psalmic tradition of Israel. Witness Psalm 2.7-9 for precisely this kind of royal ideology: 'I will tell of Yahweh's decree: He said to me, "You are my son; today I have begotten you. Ask of me, and I will make the nations your heritage, and the ends of the earth your possession. You shall break them with a rod of iron, and dash them in pieces like a potter's vessel."' The psalmist is talking about other nations who might wish to have power over Israel and make it a tributary to their nation, and he sings confidently that in fact the opposite will be the case because the king of Israel has been adopted by Yahweh as his son on the day of his coronation, and therefore other nations will become subject to Israel and will pay tribute to the Davidic monarch. In the Annals this is pictured as happening in the cases of David and Solomon, but less so in the cases of the later kings. As the Annalists tell it, the riches of the surrounding nations flow into Jerusalem.

In addition to the divine undertaking to adopt David's successor as the son of the national god, the important matter for the Annalists is that Yahweh promises, 'I will not take my steadfast love from him, as I took it from him who was before you' (v. 13). The one who was before David was Saul, and 10.13-14 gave a clear word that Yahweh had taken his steadfast love away from Saul—entirely Saul's fault, of course, because Saul had not been loyal to Yahweh and therefore Yahweh did not retain loyalty towards Saul. The hymnic recitation that 'his steadfast love endures forever' echoes a number of times in these Annals (16.34, 41; 2 Chron. 5.13; 7.3, 6; 20.21), and reference will be made on two occasions to the deity's 'steadfast love' to David (2 Chron. 1.8; 6.42); thus the word (*chesed* in Hebrew, denoting loyalty and faithfulness as much as 'love' as such) occurs often enough for us to see that it is of some significance in the Annalists' picture of how people are supposed to act over against Yahweh and how Yahweh acts over against them. We might note, though, that this oracle does not set any conditions. It does not say, 'I will take my steadfast love away from your descendants if they act as Saul acted'. It says, 'I will not take my steadfast love away from him' (v. 13), and 'I will confirm him in my house and in my kingdom forever, and his throne shall be established forever' (v. 14). An absolutely unconditional divine undertaking is made.

Well, 'forever' is a long time, but it is not literally 'forever'. The Hebrew word *olam*, which English Bibles tend to translate as 'forever', simply means an immense span of time—not technically or philosophically that there is no end to it, but that it stretches for a very long time: 'hidden time', in a sense. It is evident that the Annalists do not believe that Yahweh always has a son of David sitting on the throne, because the story that unfolds before the end of the Annals makes it clear that the kingdom ended. It may well be re-established, but it did end at a particular point. We can count up the years that the various monarchs are said in these Annals to have reigned over Israel. For example, 1 Chron. 29.27 claims that David had a 40-year reign, and 2 Chron. 9.30 claims that Solomon also had a 40-year reign (we may choose not to accept those as intentionally precise figures, but nonetheless they stand in the text). And each king that reigns after the two founding monarchs is given a figure: Rehoboam is said to have reigned for 17 years (2 Chron. 12.13), Abijah for three years (13.2), Asa for 41 years (16.13), Jehoshaphat for 25 years (20.31), Joram for eight years (21.20), and Ahaziah for one year (22.2). Athaliah is also given a figure, namely seven years (23.1), but since she is not a descendant of David, she should perhaps not be included in these figures (though her reign-span can be included if we are to make a calculation of the full length of the Davidic dynasty in the accounting of the Annalists). While Athaliah occupied the throne, young Joash was being kept in a safe place so that the Davidic monarchy could be re-established and it is said that he reigned for 40 years (24.1). Following him, the figures are given as Amaziah for 29 years (25.1), Uzziah for 52 years (26.3), Jotham for 16 years (27.1), Ahaz also for 16 years (28.1), Hezekiah for 29 years (29.1), Manasseh for 55 years (33.1), Amon for two years (33.21), Josiah for 31 years (34.1), Jehoahaz for three months (36.2), Jehoiakim for 11 years (36.5), Jehoiachin for three months (36.9), and finally Zedekiah for 11 years (36.11). If these numbers of years are added together, a grand figure of 474 years is produced. That is how long, according to the Annalists, the Davidic dynasty lasted. It is not 'forever', but it is a generation short of half a millennium—which is nonetheless an impressively long time.

But it does eventually come to an end, and the question is whether this 'forever' in the oracle they present was thought by the Annalists to imply that the Davidic dynasty would be resurrected. The fact that the genealogies (in ch. 3) trace the Davidic lineage beyond the last king of Judah through Zerubbabel (spoken of by the prophet Haggai as being active in the refounding of Jerusalem) and beyond him for many more generations suggests that these tradents do want to think of this 'forever' not simply as a vast span of half a millennium but beyond that into a time possibly without end. Because we saw that David's generation was at the halfway point of the generations that were traced in the genealogies, we can speculate that the Annalists were anticipating or hoping that the new David, the descendant of David who might reclaim this oracle, was about to appear.

David responds, affirming this 'forever'. The king appears to like the word, because he uses it several times (in vv. 23-24 and twice again in v. 27). One can readily understand why an absolute monarch might like such a concept to be applied to his hold on power, why he would be happy that it is his house that has been chosen by heaven to rule on earth. The dynastic founder links Israel and his own house inextricably: 'Yahweh of hosts, the god of Israel, is Israel's god, and the house of your servant David will be established in your presence' (v. 24). So it is inconceivable to David or to the Annalists that Israel can be firmly established (or that Yahweh's name can be firmly established) without the house of David being firmly established and magnified. Everything is very closely linked in the minds of the writers. Yahweh is David's god, and so this kingdom is both Yahweh's kingdom and David's kingdom. That slippage is noticeable even in the oracle itself, between v. 11's 'I will establish his kingdom' and v. 14's 'I will confirm him…in my kingdom'. What is David's son's kingdom is at the same time Yahweh's kingdom. The 'house' is equally intriguing, with v. 10 declaring that Yahweh 'will build you a house' and v. 14 promising that 'I will confirm him in my house'. That might mean that there will be a ceremony 'in my temple' which will confirm him, or it may be speaking of David's house as being Yahweh's house. The slippage may be deliberate, that the two are intertwined so closely in the thinking of the Annalists that we cannot really differentiate them. There can be no higher estimation of David's reign.

1 Chronicles 18–20: David's Decimation of his Foes

Chapter 18

The tale moves on swiftly now from the promises that were made in ch. 17, and in particular the one that is made that 'I will subdue all your enemies', to the fulfilment of those promises. The NRSV may slightly mislead readers with its choice of 'some time afterwards' in 18.1 and 19.1 for the Hebrew *acharey-ken*, as opposed to its use of 'after this' in 20.4 for the virtually identical *achareyken*; the former translation makes it seem that there has been quite some passage of time between the last incident and the one that is now related, but in fact the connective is a more neutral 'after this', which leaves open the possibility that the next thing happened almost immediately afterwards, and that would give us a greater sense of how the narrative voice is moving us on quickly. Perhaps the NRSV translators are influenced by the chapter divisions into thinking that more time has elapsed, but the chapter divisions are medieval inventions, not part of the ancient storytellers' artistry.

So matters move along fairly swiftly after the deity has promised the king that all his enemies will be subdued to the actual subduing of all his enemies: 'David attacked the Philistines and subdued them' (18.1). The promise made in v. 10 of the previous chapter is immediately fulfilled. We might have thought that it had been fulfilled in a sense before the divine oracle, in that David had had many excellent successes against the Philistines. But nonetheless the Philistines keep popping up from time to time; they still need to be subdued on this occasion, even if they had been put down before, and although it is recorded here that the Israelite king subdues them, we will find these quintessential enemies needing to be put down again in ch. 20.

For the moment, though, there is a great success: 'he took Gath and its villages from the Philistines'. It would seem that Gath is something of a hot spot, because we encounter that place a number of times. The first incident where the people of Gath and the people of Israel (Ephraimites in that case) had clashed was in 7.21; then 8.13 contained something similar, with other Israelites (Benjaminites this time) putting the inhabitants of Gath to flight. Thus Gath appears as a significant Philistine centre, at least in regard to the struggle with the Israelites, seen already in the genealogies and now again in the stories about David. It was noticeable too that in 13.13 a certain Obed-edom 'the Gittite' (meaning an 'inhabitant of Gath') took charge of the ark of the Israelites. Was he an Israelite who had been living under Philistine rule, a rule now broken by David? Or had the Philistines taken over Gath subsequently to the ark's sojourn there, and now David is liberating the town and its villages once again? In any event, the Gittites come on stage again in the final verses of ch. 20, where a number of warriors of Gath are seen as causing trouble for Israel. But for the moment at least David has overcome that threat.

The Philistines of 18.1 had been met with earlier in the tale (in chs. 10, 11, and 14) as the quintessential enemy, but now in v. 2 we are told that David also 'defeated Moab, and the Moabites became subject to David and brought tribute'. Apparently these Moabites are rather easily overcome, because it only takes one verse for the Annalists to introduce and bring to completion an account of David's war against Moab. There had been some brief mentions of Moab before, in the genealogies (e.g. 1.46; 4.22; 8.8) and in the account of the various people marshalling to David: 11.22 reported that one of David's champions struck down certain Moabites, so the inhabitants of Moab are to be thought of as being something of a threat or challenge. Meanwhile 11.46 listed 'Ithmah the Moabite' among David's own mighty warriors, so perhaps the Moabites had some reputation among other peoples for producing warlike qualities. No details are given about why Moab should be attacked and 'annexed' by David; similarly, even though incidents involving Moab were referred to within the genealogical material, Moab as such is not accounted for in the genealogies. We might consult Genesis 19.37 to see how the ancient Israelites classified the Moabite people among others, but the Annalists do not bother to catalogue them.

The little scroll of Ruth, which forms part of our Hebrew Bible, offers a fascinating angle, because it talks about a certain Moabite woman who marries into the Israelite nation and indeed becomes the great-great-grandmother of none less than David himself. We are told nothing about that in these Annals. Was that legend known to the Annalists? In 2.12 the Annals provide the genealogy of Boaz, who married the Moabite woman Ruth according to the book of Ruth, but there is no mention of Ruth herself in the Annalists' genealogy. The scroll's insistence that David's great-great-grandmother is a Moabitess (Ruth 1.4, 22; 2.2, 6, 21; 4.5, 10) clashes with the legal stipulation in Deuteronomy 23.3 that 'no Ammonite or Moabite shall be admitted to the assembly of Yahweh; even to the tenth generation, none of their descendants shall be admitted to the assembly of Yahweh' (and the ruthless policy in Ezra 10.3 of driving out of Jerusalem the children of marriages with Moabite and other non-Israelite women). Under such a law, David himself ought not to be allowed into the assembly. So it is not surprising that, if the Annalists knew of the scroll of Ruth and its contention that Israel's founding monarch was descended from a Moabite, then they suppressed the story and did not include any allusion to it in their Annals. It could be a rather embarrassing admission, so instead we have David defeating the Moabites and certainly no mention that he may be related to them.

Readers might speculate on why David attacks the Moabites after subduing the Philistines. Perhaps the Moabites are to be thought of as flexing their muscles on the Israelite border and so the Israelite king needs to overcome the threat they represented, or perhaps David himself is to be thought of as an expansionist and the Israelites themselves as being in the business of taking over the territories of others without provocation from them. There is some indication in the genealogies that it is indeed the case in this story-world that the Israelites want more territory for themselves (4.39-43; 5.9-10, 19-22), but in any event the perceived benefits of having tribute paid into one's coffers are readily imagined. And so it is that Moab becomes the first of the surrounding nations that will bring tribute to David (18.2). Not long afterwards we are told that plunder is brought in 'from Edom, Moab, the Ammonites, the Philistines, and Amalek' (v. 11). Some details are given immediately of the conquest of the Edomites (vv. 12-13), and then later a more complicated account of how the Ammonites came to be vanquished is related (ch. 19). No information is given about defeating 'Amalek' or the Amalekites, while other peoples not mentioned in the summary of 18.11 do have appearances in the surrounding stories, particularly various groups of Arameans. In 18.5 'the Arameans of Damascus came to help King Hadadezer of Zobah', but meanwhile the people of Hamath apparently did not ally themselves with the people of Zobah (vv. 9-10). In 19.6 King Hanun of Ammon is aided by 'the Arameans of the two rivers' (NRSV 'Mesopotamia') and 'the Arameans of Maacah' (NRSV 'Aram-maacah'). These territories lie to the north and east of Israel in what we might, broadly speaking, call the Syrian and Lebanese regions, but the account of the battles goes further south as well, into Ammonite and Moabite territory.

Some figures are given for various numbers of chariots and men involved in these battles, and huge figures for the numbers of people killed. In 18.5, for example, it is noted that David killed 22,000 Arameans. Further figures are given in 18.12 (18,000 Edomites), 19.18 (47,000 Arameans) and 20.4-7 (a number of individual warriors). If all those figures are added up, no less than 87,000 people are killed, plus a few extras that are named: certain Philistine champions from Gath and related regions as well as certain commanders of the army. But 87,000 battle-deaths is a staggering figure and looks to be an inflated statistic for the purpose of demonstrating how phenomenal was David's success. No matter how huge the armies that were ranged against him, he was still able to overcome them because Yahweh was on his side.

The figures that are spelled out do not include the people that are enslaved. In 19.19, for example, mention is made of a certain group that David had subjected to his rule, and already several times in ch. 18 (vv. 2, 4, 6, 13) various peoples were mentioned as becoming enslaved or subject to him. In 20.3 the same expression is not used, but just what this enslavement might mean is spelled out a little more: 'He brought out the people who were in [that particular city] and set them to work with saws and iron picks and axes; thus David did to all the cities of the Ammonites'. If the ones that were enslaved were added to those that were killed, even more phenomenal numbers would be produced. Note too the expression in 20.1, where Joab, David's commander, 'ravaged the country of the Ammonites, and came and besieged Rabbah'. The numbers killed and raped and injured in various ways in that war are not recounted, but it is certainly not a pretty picture that is being painted in these chapters, even though the storytellers probably want us to think that it *is* a pretty picture, in the sense that we are no doubt supposed to cheer the great successes of David. Perhaps we are meant to think that all of these neighbouring peoples are warlike nations that need to be subjugated and have their wealth flowing into Jerusalem, and therefore we are meant to think that this is all a very good thing. Nevertheless, underneath all this there is a very dark side to the narrative, which seems to take it for granted that it is good for David that various tribute is brought to him, and it is good for the temple of Yahweh, since materials that are thus brought in will be useful for its construction and outfitting. A note about that is already given not long after the delivery of the divine words 'one of your sons...shall build a house for me' (17.11-12): 18.8 notes that 'David took a vast amount of bronze' from the cities that he had conquered, and 'with it Solomon made the bronze sea and the pillars and the vessels of bronze'. Thus we are told that Solomon will build the temple from the material that David is now accumulating. Accordingly, in this narrative of warfare and death and destruction there is a note that the warrior god who is fighting for David will himself directly benefit from all this conquest, in the building of his temple.

Details of 'the bronze sea and the pillars and the vessels of bronze' can be consulted later in the Annals. 2 Chronicles 4.2-6 is concerned with 'the bronze sea', the large basin of water in which the priests wash themselves; because they are very much involved with bloodshed in the temple, with all the animals that they sacrifice ('22,000 oxen and 120,000 sheep' are offered up on one day alone in 2 Chron. 7.5), the priests need a large area in which to wash themselves and to clean all that blood off themselves. 2 Chronicles 3.15-17 is concerned with 'the pillars', the two columns that stand at the front of the temple and that are given personal names of presumably some significance (although we cannot tell quite what the significance is). And 2 Chron. 4.16 is concerned with 'the vessels of bronze'. But for the moment we only have a brief note that 'a vast quantity of bronze' (1 Chron. 18.8) will be useful in temple building, that David is already starting to gather the material for a temple. We also have here a mention that 'Solomon' (v. 8) is the one that is going to bring the plans to fruition. Up until that reference there was very little indication as to which of David's sons will inherit his throne; the dynastic oracle had simply promised the founding monarch a son who would succeed him, and he had many sons. Who would it be? Even after this naming of 'Solomon' in v. 8, v. 17 says 'David's sons were the chief officials in the service of the king'—again no indication there that Solomon is to emerge in some way from among these sons. Later too we will not be told how it is that Solomon came to inherit the throne when David had so many sons—and so many of them were indeed older than Solomon. We will simply be told that Yahweh chose Solomon to be the king after David.

In v. 10 the Annalists relate that King Tou of Hamath sends various articles to David; not just the bronze that will be used for the temple building, but also gold and silver, which can be similarly used but which also make fine possessions for a king. Why is Tou sending all that material to the king of Israel when he has not been an ally of King Hadadezer of Zobah and therefore has not been defeated by Israel? He represents himself in fact as having been against Zobah. So is it simply out of gratitude that he sends this to Jerusalem, or is it an insurance policy—the realization that he had better pay tribute to King David too, or the same thing will happen to him? It is preferable to pay tribute up front, rather than to have your country desolated and all of your wealth taken away from you. One wonders, though, how this present that he sends to David in v. 10 differs from the tribute that he would have been paying previously to Hadadezer. It seems that he has really just swapped one master for another, but, if it has secured his country from being ravaged as the Ammonite territory will later be ravaged, then it may well be a price worth paying.

In vv. 12-13 it is the Edomites who feel David's might, and again nothing in the Annals has really prepared readers for this particular battle; that is, nothing has been said about Edom threatening Israel or being part of an anti-Israelite alliance or the like. Actually the Edomites are the legendary enemies from the book of Genesis, and readers might be expected to know something of the stories about the two brothers Jacob (who is also known as 'Israel') and Esau (who is also known as 'Edom'): they fight with each other, and eventually have a kind of uneasy *rapprochement*, but there continues to be friction between the descendants of these two eponymous ancestors. We are not told details of that in the Annals; in fact we are not told explicitly that Esau and Edom are the same person. It is made clear in Genesis (particularly in Genesis 36.1), and in the Annalists' genealogies certain references like 1 Chron. 1.34 make it reasonably clear that the Edomites are descendants of Esau, so readers are probably expected to have some such notion in the back of their minds when they read this episode about the king of Israel overcoming the people of Edom. And overcome them he does: they 'became subject to' or 'became enslaved by' David (v. 13) after several thousands of them have been put to death by 'Abishai son of Zeruiah' (v. 12). Notice in v. 15 another son of Zeruiah, Joab, is the top commander. Later (in 19.10-11) we are told how the army of David is divided for military purposes under those two brothers, Abishai and Joab, in a very successful manoeuvre. But it is the Edomites who are at the end of the Israelite swords at this stage, and once again Yahweh gives 'victory to David wherever he went' (v. 13, exactly as was said in v. 6). There are no decisive losses for David; victory follows him wherever he goes, because Yahweh is giving him the victory.

'So David reigned over all Israel' (v. 14), a nation mightily expanded as a result of now having various tributary nations on all sides apart from the south. There is now a buffer zone all around David's kingdom, and the tribute of these surrounding nations is flowing in. 'And he administered justice and equity to all his people' (v. 14). One might wonder whether all of those enforced slaves of these verses think that he is administering justice and equity to them, but they are probably not 'his people' and therefore not part of this 'justice and equity'. No judges, an office we might regard as important for justice to be administered, are mentioned in the list of the kingdom's functionaries in vv. 15-17. Pride of place in this list goes to the commander of the army, as the army is the most important part of the system. It is the army that brings all this wealth from the surrounding peoples to David and his kingdom, and it is also the army that can be trusted to keep the people of Israel under control, just in case there is anyone who thinks that the king's 'justice and equity' is not helping them.

Next after army commander 'Joab son of Zeruiah' is listed 'Jehoshaphat son of Ahilud', who is 'recorder' (*mazkir*, from a verb meaning 'to remember' [*zakar*]). The office-holder so designated could be someone who takes down all of the king's business, who keeps an account of what has been decided or judged by the king and therefore must be obeyed, a 'recorder of legislation'. If such an individual is chief interpreter and enforcer of the law, it is a very powerful office indeed.

After the two figures of v. 15, we have (in v. 16) two priests, Zadok and Ahimelech, and Shavsha the 'secretary'. In modern parlance we might say 'secretary of state'; the Hebrew word *sopher* (from the verb *saphar*, 'to count') denotes a registrar, accountant, or scribe, and in this context presumably designates a high official of state, not simply a minute-secretary or low-ranking official. Nevertheless, we can note in passing that the word *sopher* can mean someone who keeps a record of numbers, and so might designate a census or taxation official (which might have some relevance for ch. 21, where David is pictured as counting the people).

The list of named functionaries in David's kingdom is rounded off in v. 17 with 'Benaiah son of Jehoiada over the Cherethites and the Pelethites'. This is the only mention of these groups in the Annals. We are not told who they are or what they do, but, in view of the context in which they appear, they presumably have something to do with military matters or with the bureaucratic running of the kingdom. Are they enforcers of some kind? The name 'Cherethite' may be connected with the island of Crete, and thus designate a person from Crete; so too 'Pelethite' might designate another ethnic group. The possibility, then, is that they are foreign mercenaries, perhaps an elite bodyguard of foreigners, persons who bear no allegiance to the house of Saul or any other tribe in Israel, but allegiance only to the man who pays their wages—and pays them quite handsomely, one might assume—namely David himself. This is speculation, because we are told nothing about them. The word *kreti* ('Cherethite') may or may not refer to a Cretan; it appears to stem from the Hebrew verb *karat*, 'to cut', and thus the people so designated may be 'the cutters, the enforcers', those who have ways of making you do what they want you to do. There is no Hebrew verb attested in the Bible to which *pleti* ('Pelethite') might be related, but there is a possible Arabic cognate which means 'swiftness'. Thus the Pelethites could be the elite front-line troops, perhaps the specialist cavalry—or they could be the secret police, swiftly dispatched wherever dissidents might be.

These speculations see in 'the Cherethites and the Pelethites' a crucial element in running an organization such as David's, where there may be some opposition to his rule. The Annalists have suggested that 'all Israel' is loyal to their new king, but at the same time they have given some indications that perhaps not 'all' are with David. But quite apart from the Israelites, David is now controlling vast numbers of non-Israelites who would presumably rebel at any opportunity, so perhaps these Cherethites and Pelethites are responsible for border patrols and keeping the non-Israelites in place rather than (or in addition to) internal patrols and keeping the Israelites under control. On the other hand, they might after all be people who are involved in welfare work or the kind of really nice things that governments do when they seek to look after the well-being of their citizens. No details are given, so nothing can be said for certain about what the Annalists believe these groups to be.

Chapter 19

As ch. 19 begins, King Nahash of the Ammonites comes to the end of his life and his son succeeds him. Again there are no details about Ammon in the Annals, just a mention in 11.39, so readers would need to refer to Genesis 19.38 to see how the Ammonites were thought (by at least some ancient Hebrew tradents) to relate to the Israelites, just as it would be necessary to refer to Genesis 19.37 for the Moabites. According to Genesis, the Moabites and Ammonites are very closely related peoples, and also related to the Israelites. But now in the Annals of King David, with King Nahash of the Ammonites having died, his son Hanun (named in v. 2) apparently does not want to be paying tribute to David and does a dastardly deed to David's servants. One might think that his officials are rightly suspicious in what they say (in v. 3), given what David has been doing to the surrounding nations and to the Moabites right next door to the Ammonites. But nonetheless, even if they have grounds for such suspicion, it is a rather foolish action that their greenhorn king carries out, shaving David's emissaries and cutting off their garments in the middle at their hips. Incidentally, the verb in 19.4 for 'cutting off' the garments is the same verb (*karat*) as that to be found in the name Cherethites ('the cutters'?) mentioned a little while ago, although these are not Cherethites in action but Ammonites, and David is very angry about it. Nonetheless, he bides his time, and instructs his emissaries to stay in Jericho until their beards have grown, a policy which suggests that for a grown man not to have a beard is a matter of some shame and that these personnel will naturally want to grow their beards back before they appear in public again. Of course having their garments cut off at their hips, thus revealing a certain part of their anatomy, is also a matter of shame, but a man can soon put on a new pair of clothes once he is away from the people who have deprived him of half of his garment, whereas it takes somewhat longer for him to grow a respectable beard.

The Ammonites realize soon after perpetrating this act that it was a very foolhardy scheme, given that the powerful king of Israel is on their doorstep, and so they hire chariots and cavalry from the Aramean kingdom of Maacah to help defend themselves. No less than the staggering figure of '32,000 chariots' (v. 7) are secured, and at the cost of '1000 talents of silver'—one wonders if it would have been cheaper simply to have paid tribute to Jerusalem. Among the soldiers they hire are people from Zobah (v. 6), a nation David had already defeated (in ch. 18), so it seems that the Zobahites are still able and willing to muster some chariots even after David had had almost all of their horses hamstrung (as we were told in 18.4). Troops from Zobah will appear later in 19.16 ('the servants of Hadadezer', the defeated ruler of Zobah), so the Zobahites are nothing if not resilient. However, they are no match for the tactics of Joab and his brother Abishai, who divide the Israelite army into two forces. The prospect of two fronts might be thought to stack the odds somewhat against Israel, but of course Israel has Yahweh on their side, as Joab implies in v. 13 ('may Yahweh do what seems good to him'). Joab's expression that his men are fighting 'for our people and for the cities of our god' is interesting in this context of Ammonite opposition. Are we to understand that the city outside of which this battle was taking place, which is named as Medeba in v. 7, is a city of Yahweh? It lies, after all, in the land of Moab. But certain ancient Hebrew traditions—as represented in Numbers 32.1-5, 34-38 (where Medeba is not named, but other cities in that region are)—give the impression that Israel regarded these areas as part of their rightful inheritance, and so Joab may be depicted as fighting for Israelite cities even when they are Moabite cities.

What 'seems good' to Yahweh is obviously to give victory to David's forces, and so vv. 14-15 depict various people fleeing before the Israelite troops. Notice the repetition of 'fled' (Hebrew *nus*) in 'they *fled* before [Joab], and when the Ammonites saw that the Arameans *fled*, they likewise *fled* before Abishai'. The same kind of repetition had been seen in the Israelites fleeing from the Philistines in 10.1, 7. Thus once again readers are provided with a little narrative reminder that David is successful where Saul was not. Actually, David was not at the battle; at that stage he was quite happy for his generals, his close relatives Joab and Abishai, to be leading the troops. But when more Arameans are brought forward from the Aramean heartland as reinforcements (v. 16), then the Israelite king himself (v. 17) gathers 'all Israel' together and crosses the Jordan to engage the accumulated enemy forces in a decisive battle. Once the major group of Arameans has come from beyond the Euphrates, then David and no less than David must go out to fight them. After they 'fled before Israel' (v. 18), there are no further groups of Arameans to come forward. There is no one 'willing' to do it anymore, as v. 19 says. Verse 16 had begun, 'When the Arameans saw that they had been defeated by Israel…', and now v. 19 begins, 'When the servants of Hadadezer saw that they had been defeated by Israel…', but rather different responses are seen on these two occasions. In the earlier verse the protagonists thought to bring reinforcements from their heartland, but that did not work, and so in the later verse they sue for peace. It is peace through defeat and fear, as the imperial imposition of peace so often is, but nonetheless it is peace. The storytellers are moving us towards the period of rest that is necessary for the temple to be built.

Chapter 20

We have not quite reached that period of rest necessary for thoughts to turn fully to the temple project, because ch. 20 has more battles. Indeed v. 1 begins, 'In the spring of the year, the time when kings go out to battle', telling us that warfare is a regular occurrence; there is a season for war. It is a rather distressing idea, that kings might think that what they have to do each springtime is to mount ravaging expeditions against other nations, but such is the notion implied by the phrasing of the Annals. So Joab leads out the army on his king's behalf (20.1), as he had done before (19.8). We are not told why this mission is against the country of the Ammonites. Perhaps they have not paid the tribute they ought to have paid. They had been defeated in the previous chapter, but apparently they still need to be subdued, for Joab leads the army to the Ammonite capital city of Rabbah and overthrows it. At first David remains in Jerusalem, as he had done during the initial forays against the Ammonites (19.8). But then it is said that 'David took the crown of their king from his head' and 'brought out the booty of the city' (20.2) and that subsequently 'David and all the people returned to Jerusalem' (v. 3), so one assumes that when the campaign got to the decisive point at which it is necessary for the supreme commander of the forces to be there, then he went.

The NRSV reads v. 2 as 'David took the crown of Milcom from his head', but actually the Hebrew account reads 'David took the crown of *their king (malkam)* from his head' and does not name the king or his crown. An Ammonite king had been named in 19.2, namely Hanun son of Nahash, so perhaps it is still that rebellious monarch at this point. More likely, readers should think that Hanun had been killed or deposed in the earlier conflict and somebody else had taken the throne by this stage (or perhaps that a different monarch rules in the city of Rabbah in any event), but whatever the king's name, he is no match for David, who takes the crown from his head and has it placed on his own head. Once again something from the episode of Saul may be recalled, namely Saul's head being removed and taken away by the Philistines, 'head' being a word that can obviously symbolize the rulership of the country. David's head is firmly attached to his body, and the crowns of other, subjugated kings are placed on his head. Perhaps the head of the king of Rabbah was removed, as was Saul's, but we are not specifically told that. What we are specifically told is another Annalistic exaggeration: that this crown 'weighed a talent of gold' (v. 2). A 'talent' (Hebrew *kikar*) is something like 34 kg or 75 lbs, which is rather heavy for a human head to support, but David's head is evidently up to the task.

In v. 3 David brings out the people and sets them to work 'with saws and iron picks and axes'. The work may be the rebuilding of the city of Rabbah, if it has been destroyed in the attack by Joab's troops—these ancient stories often seem to depict a rather distressing cycle of destroying and rebuilding. But it may not be that he is asking them to rebuild their own city; he might not particularly care if their city is in ruins. It may be that he wants them to make goods for his own city, and rather than transport the manufactured goods to Jerusalem, he may deport the workers themselves to that city.

In any event, in vv. 4-8 we have something of a return to how the David story began, with an account of his mighty men and their exploits against various antagonists. Time and again war is depicted as breaking out with the Philistines (three particular battles are itemized in vv. 4, 5, and 6). The Israelites and the Philistines clash regularly, it seems, perhaps every springtime (or at least for three springtimes) if we take seriously v. 1's contention that spring is 'the time when kings go out to battle'. Three particular contests between champions are mentioned in relation to these campaigns: 'Sibbecai the Hushathite killed Sippai' (v. 4), 'Elhanan son of Jair killed Lahmi the brother of Goliath the Gittite' (v. 5), and 'Jonathan son of Shimea, David's brother, killed' an unnamed 'man of great size' (vv. 6-7). These Philistine champions are reputed to be 'descended from the giants' (vv. 4, 6, 8), if we take the Hebrew words *rephaim* (v. 4) and *rapha* (vv. 6, 8) as meaning people of great stature (a translation supported by an understanding of the expression 'man of great size' [*ish middah*] in v. 6 as being a parallel depiction), though the words could also be translated as 'ghosts' or even as 'healers'—they are words with some slippage in classical Hebrew, employed to indicate figures of legendary dimensions or of not fully human form. Here, the use of an expression indicating that the shaft of Lahmi's spear was 'like a weaver's beam' (v. 5), the same expression as was used of the spear of an Egyptian opponent of another of David's champions in the earlier episodes (11.23), suggests that we are talking about figures of great dimensions. But David's men are up to the challenge. These exploits in 20.4-8 as a group echo the exploits of the heroes of David in 11.11-25. Once again the Philistines are 'subdued', as v. 4 has it. From time to time, it seems, they rise up just a little, but are easily subdued once more. Although they will still raise their heads again a little later in the piece, by this stage David has achieved the domination over Israel's antagonists that is needed for the next dramatic episode in his story.

1 Chronicles 21: David's Tabulation of his Troops

The 'satanic verse' of Chronicles (1 Chron. 21.1) might startle a modern English reader, for suddenly it is said (in the NRSV) that 'Satan stood up against Israel, and incited David to count the people of Israel'. There has been no sign of a satanic presence in the narrative up to this point, and there will be no further appearance of such an entity as the Annals unfold, but for a short sharp moment he stands in the text, inviting scrutiny.

Some readers' thoughts will immediately fly to an image painted vividly in the New Testament and more particularly in medieval Christendom, of a devilish creature who stands against all that is good and holy, a cosmic force that battles with God for control of the universe but is destined for eventual defeat at the close of the age. Yet it is most unlikely that the Annalists imagined a being of that apocalyptic kind, since no such colours are to be seen on their canvas: just this one enigmatic verse, in which someone or something prompts the king of Israel into an undertaking which will have certain repercussions, at first terrible (the ravages of plague throughout the nation) but ultimately wonderful (the designation of the site for the national temple).

Who is this 'Satan' who suddenly appears in and just as suddenly disappears from the Annals of King David? In point of fact, he does not appear to be 'Satan' at all, in the sense of later Jewish and Christian theological developments concerning a Grand Opponent of God, but rather 'a satan', in the sense of an adversary or opponent on a much more modest scale. The Hebrew word *satan* simply means 'adversary', and so it appears in a number of strands of ancient Hebrew tradition, both in stories (Numbers 22.22: 'the angel of Yahweh took his stand in the road as a satan to him' [NRSV 'as his adversary']) and in hymns (Psalm 109.6: 'appoint a wicked man against him; let a satan [NRSV 'an accuser'] stand on his right'). In the Chronicles passage, too, an English rendering would best avoid the loaded English term 'Satan' and simply translate the verse as 'An adversary stood up against Israel, and incited David to count Israel'. The Annalists may be saying no more than that the king received adverse counsel (that is to say, advice which ran counter to the best interests of the nation), upon which he was persuaded to undertake a census of his people, even though another counsellor (Joab, in v. 3) argues strenuously against the plan as soon as he is apprised of it.

(As to the satanic nature of the figure in question in v. 1, it should be pointed out that even in the two strands of formative Hebrew tradition where a *satan* is a more fleshed-out character and seems to be given the word as a kind of title, *hassatan* or 'the satan', readers of what came to be Hebrew biblical texts will find nothing approaching a fully fledged Devil running amok against the purposes of the divine will. In Job 1.6–2.7, one of the members of the heavenly council carries the designation 'the satan' and appears to be 'the prosecuting attorney', an angel who is assigned the role of putting forward the case against particular mortals. And in Zechariah 3.1-2, a prophetic vision is presented in which the divine judge refuses to accept an accusation brought against the high priest by 'the satan', again apparently functioning as a kind of prosecuting attorney. But in any case the one brief mention in Chronicles of 'a satan' leading an earthly monarch astray seems far removed from the heavenly courtroom scenes depicted in Job and Zechariah.)

There is yet a second mystery about the very first verse in the census episode: the clear signal given by the narrators that for the king 'to count Israel' (NRSV 'to count the people of Israel') is no good thing. Readers of these Annals might find that value-judgment rather more startling than the discovery that there was 'an adversary' in David's court. After all, there has been a great deal of counting underlying the pages of this book. Figures were enumerated for example in 7.2 ('their number in the days of David was 22,600') and 7.40 ('their number…was 26,000'), and in 12.23-38 many sets of numbers were given of those who came to David to make him king. Accordingly it hardly seems that the Annalists are opposed in principle to counting Israelites. On the contrary, they seem to have a distinct liking for counting Israelites, for there is more to come in ch. 27, where the tabulations are introduced by the words 'the children of Israel, according to their number' (27.1 [NRSV 'this is the list of the people of Israel']), without any suggestion that setting out 'their number' is a sinful thing to do, whereas in the present episode there is a strong implication that the king is sinning in wanting to 'know their number' (21.2).

Verse 2 may already suggest why this royal decree is to be condemned, in that David issues his orders without any ado—that is, without consulting either the deity directly (as in 14.10) or an intermediary acting on the deity's behalf (as in 17.1)—and that the orders are issued 'to Joab and the commanders of the army'. This latter detail could be construed innocently enough, since the army might be the only agency capable of operating a census throughout the kingdom, no matter what the precise purpose of such a census, but equally the implication could be drawn from the immediate mobilization of military commanders that the king has a military purpose in view. If so, and despite the Annalists' reticence to spell it out at this point in the drama, such a royal scheme would go against certain ideas that are expressed elsewhere in the Annals. In 2 Chron. 16.7-9 a seer (Hanani) is presented as saying to a descendant of David (King Asa), 'Because you relied on the king of Aram, and did not rely on your god Yahweh, the army of the king of Aram has escaped you. Were not the Ethiopians and the Libyans a huge army with exceedingly very many chariots and cavalry? Yet because you relied on Yahweh, he gave them into your hand. For the eyes of Yahweh range throughout the entire earth, to strengthen those whose heart is true to him. You have done foolishly in this; for from now on you will have wars.'

Is the implication in 1 Chronicles 21 therefore that David is not relying on Yahweh, that he is trying to make an assessment of how many troops he has in order to plan his future strategy accordingly? Against this the prophet later speaking in 2 Chronicles 16 implies that the numbers in the Israelite army are immaterial: if the people of Israel rely on their deity rather than their own human strength, then they will be successful, but if they do not rely on Yahweh, then, no matter how many troops they have, they will not be successful. Something rather similar to that is also to be found in a prophetic tradition represented in Isaiah 31.1: 'Alas for those who go down to Egypt for help and who rely on horses, who trust in chariots because they are many and in horsemen because they are very strong, but do not look to the Holy One of Israel, or consult Yahweh!' That would seem to be what David is doing wrong here, in the judgment of these writers: he is not consulting Yahweh. He is not even consulting his officials (whom he had talked to about his plan to move the sacred ark to Jerusalem) or the prophet Nathan (whom he had talked to when he had it in mind to build a house for his god). He simply gets this new idea in his head and immediately instructs the military to carry it out.

There is another possible hint within the book of Chronicles itself as to what is supposed to be wrong with counting the people, and that is in 1 Chron. 27.23-24, where the comment is made that 'David did not count those below 20 years of age, for Yahweh had promised to make Israel as numerous as the stars of heaven. Joab son of Zeruiah began to count them, but did not finish; yet wrath came upon Israel for this, and the number was not entered into the account of the Annals of King David.' That chapter has to do with an accounting of the Levites in particular, but again the implication may be more generally that it is not right to count these people whose magnitude was the subject of a divine undertaking. That would be in a sense testing Yahweh, or trying to find out if the deity has indeed done what he had promised. Of course the god of Israel would do what he had promised, and he may not take kindly to someone wanting to see hard evidence. He was on record in Israelite tradition (as told in Genesis 22.17 and 26.4) as initially promising the patriarch Abraham that his offspring would become 'as numerous as the stars of heaven and as the sand that is on the seashore'. But we might also note the strongly worded threat in Deuteronomy 28.62-63: 'Although once you were as numerous as the stars in heaven, you shall be left few in number, because you did not obey your god Yahweh. And just as Yahweh took delight in making you prosperous and numerous, so Yahweh will take delight in bringing you to ruin and destruction.' That in its context is a prediction of the exile, but nonetheless may be relevant in the context of 1 Chronicles 21. Certainly it is said quite clearly that David is doing something wrong, for in v. 3 Joab's response is that the king will 'bring guilt on Israel' by counting the people. Joab says, 'May Yahweh increase the number of his people a hundredfold!' (and by implication, therefore, 'Do not count them, my lord the king!').

The king's word prevails and the army does count the Israelites, with Joab giving the count to David in v. 5: 'In all Israel there were 1,100,000 men who drew the sword, and in Judah 470,000 men who drew the sword'. There are two things to note about this. Firstly, it is 'men who drew the sword' who are counted, which seems to imply that it is military preparation that is happening, rather than simply taxation or any other reason for which a royal authority might wish to know the numbers of citizens in the kingdom. The other thing to notice is the figure of 1,100,000. Adult men, or the men who are able to perform military service, are presumably about one third of the population, and so '1,100,000 men' would mean that the Annalists are imagining that the census revealed well in excess of 3,000,000 inhabitants—a quite staggering figure for David's era. It is a remarkable figure even within the imaginary world of the Annalists, for it is a threefold increase on the figures that they presented in ch. 12, when readers were told of the fighting men from all Israel who came to David. A total figure was not given in that earlier setting, but when the respective tribal numbers are added up it amounts to a picture of 340,000 'men who drew the sword' coming to David 'from all Israel...to make David king'. Now in ch. 21 with 1,100,000 we find three times that number. In Judah, David's own tribe, matters are even more remarkable in that the figure of 470,000 who draw the sword in 21.5 represents a seventyfold increase over the mere 6800 armed troops in 12.24. This is not quite the hundredfold increase of which Joab speaks hyperbolically in v. 3, but it is highly impressive nonetheless.

The Levites and Benjaminites are not included in the numbering, according to v. 6. They were included in the numbering in ch. 12, where counts of 8300 from Levi and 3000 from Benjamin are given, but for Joab to have included them on this occasion would have been 'abhorrent'. No explanation is provided for the particular abhorrence of counting these two tribes, but reasons may be supposed. In the case of Benjamin, the tribe from which the displaced King Saul arose, it might be thought that they are not yet loyal to the new king and accordingly, as they cannot be counted upon to fight for David, they are not included in this particular numbering. But we were told in ch. 12 that various Benjaminites were among those—and indeed among the first—who came to David to make him king. Another explanation might be that because the tabernacle at Gibeon is in Benjaminite territory the services of the Benjaminites are required there to protect the tabernacle and so none of that vital section of the Israelite fighting forces should be drawn into whatever other military strategy (such as leaving Israelite territory to pursue conquests of neighbouring peoples) is being hatched by David on this occasion. And the Levites, as the tribe of priests, are presumably not to be counted either. Indeed, in Numbers 1.49 it is stipulated that Levites are not to be numbered, at least not for military purposes. They are numbered in Numbers 3.15, but presumably for a purpose other than a military one, namely to organize them for the functioning of the temple (or at that stage the tabernacle). So too later in the Annals we will see them numbered and listed in genealogies in order to arrange for the proper functioning of the temple. On the other hand there is a significant armed aspect of the Levites in those later chapters, and indeed already in 1 Chronicles 12 the Levites were numbered among the fighting men with no adverse comment being made about that by the Annalists, but Joab will not have that here and refuses to include them in this counting.

Even so, that does not save Israel from its god's wrath: 'the deity was displeased with this thing, and he struck Israel' (v. 7). Previously he had mostly confined himself to striking Israel's enemies, as in 14.15, where he was pictured as striking down the Philistines on behalf of the Israelites, and indeed it was implied that the Philistines could not have been subdued if Israel's god had not been doing the striking. Israel by itself, without divine aid, was not strong enough to conquer Philistia, in the view of the Annalists, whose present chapter perhaps suggests that David was now thinking for a moment or two that the Israelites could fight their own battles under his astute leadership. Yet even under David's leadership this incident is not the first time that Yahweh has been depicted as striking against someone in Israel, for in 13.10 the unfortunate Uzzah was struck down for having the audacity to touch the ark of Yahweh, as though the deity required help to keep his ark on an even keel during its journey from Kiriath-jearim to Jerusalem. Now that same god strikes Israel because of the king's personal offence against him, arguably an analogous one in contemplating the military might of Israel without reference to its god.

David quickly confesses, 'I have sinned greatly in that I have done this thing' (v. 8). The narrative sequence seems to imply that his god had already 'struck Israel' (v. 7) and that that was the cause of the king's belief that he had brought guilt upon the nation, in accordance with the traditional view that the national god brought bad things upon the people whenever their king had acted badly. If some indication of the divine displeasure had already occurred, worse is to come, but the deity does not give a direct answer to the royal confession, preferring to speak through an intermediary. In the episode of ch. 17 it had been the prophet Nathan who spoke to David, but on that occasion the king had initiated the conversation with the prophet. This time David had neglected to consult with any prophet about his plans, and now when he speaks to his god (v. 8), his god speaks to Gad (v. 9), and Gad speaks to the king (v. 11).

This new intermediary—'Gad, David's seer'—has not been seen in the story before v. 9, and he will not be seen again after v. 19, when the king follows his instructions to the letter. In the Davidic story told in these pages Gad is a seer who speaks directly only once (vv. 11-12) and then just once more indirectly on a follow-up exercise (v. 18), although the Annalists will mention both him and Nathan again in 1 Chron. 29.29 and 2 Chron. 29.25 as people who kept royal records and issued divine decrees during the time of David (and of course a tribal group called 'Gad' is mentioned several times). On all three occasions when the Annalists introduce a reference to this intermediary, they refer to him as a 'seer' (*chozeh*, as in v. 9), whereas Nathan is termed a 'prophet' (*nabi*, as in 17.1), but since Nathan's prophetic activity is also depicted in terms of that functionary having been given a 'vision' (*chazon*, 17.15), there is probably no implication of different roles between these two individuals. They appear as simply the two major professional prophets associated with David's reign, practitioners able to provide oracles for the royal service. The Annalists presumably think of the one as being active earlier in the reign and the other later (this may be implied by the sequence of 'Samuel...Nathan...Gad' in 29.29, reflecting the brief appearances of the three men in 11.3, 17.1-15 and 21.9-13 respectively), but the alert reader will remember that earlier in the Davidic adventure the Annalists wrote as if David was speaking directly to his god and that same god was responding directly to him without the need for any intermediary (for example in 14.10, where 'David inquired of the deity, "Shall I go up against the Philistines? Will you give them into my hand?", and Yahweh said to him, "Go up, and I will give them into your hand"'). That is certainly no longer the case by the time we come to these episodes in which first Nathan and now Gad appear on the scene as spokesmen for divinity, although it might be argued that the Annalists are simply giving a more detailed account in these later episodes and so we should assume that professional intermediaries were also understood to have been involved in the earlier episodes.

Now Gad brings to David a word of Yahweh, in which the king is offered a choice of three punishments: one lasting for three years, one lasting for three months, and one lasting for three days. It seems that the Annalists have some fondness for threes, since there are several episodes in their Annals that involve threefold periods of time, such as the three days of blessings in 1 Chron. 12.39, the three months of blessings in 1 Chron. 13.14, and the three years of blessings in 2 Chron. 11.17 (not to mention the repetitions and confusions of threes and thirties in the adventures of 1 Chron. 11). Here the three threefold periods are not of blessings but of curses, either 'famine' or 'devastation' or 'pestilence' (v. 12).

The latter two choices involve the alternatives of 'the sword of your [human] enemies' on the one hand and 'the sword of Yahweh' as a kind of divine enemy on the other. The king chooses the heavenly adversary rather than earthly adversaries, saying (in v. 13), 'Let me fall into the hand of Yahweh, for his mercy is very great; but let me not fall into human hands'. He seems to have forgotten about the first offer, 'famine', which one would suppose is also an Act of God rather than the actions of human enemies, but that alternative involves the longest period of time, three years. The king chooses the shortest form of punishment: 'pestilence', or 'three days of the sword of Yahweh', in preference to 'three months of...the sword of your enemies'. These two sets of swords in v. 12 hark back to the enumeration in v. 5 of so-and-so-many Israelites 'who drew the sword' and so-and-so-many Judahites 'who drew the sword'. The punishment fits the crime: the king was in his counting-house, counting how many people could draw the sword, and the deity responds by drawing a sword of his own against those people. The traditional Hebrew justice system laid down 'an eye for an eye, a tooth for a tooth... a wound for a wound' (Exodus 21.24-25), so 'a sword-strike for a sword-strike' matches well (or as a later teacher might put it, 'those who take the sword will perish by the sword' [Matthew 26.52]).

This sword of Yahweh cuts down 70,000 people (v. 14), which represents one in every 16 of the Israelites who had been counted in the king's survey (v. 5), so the 'swords' in their human hands were as nothing compared to the 'sword' in the divine hand—or in the hand of the divine agent sent to do the actual dirty work: 'the angel of Yahweh standing between earth and heaven, and in his hand a drawn sword' (v. 16). The narrative sequence in vv. 14-16, with tens of thousands of people succumbing to the pestilence 'in Israel' and then the destroying angel moving towards Jerusalem to destroy it but stopping with his sword 'stretched out over Jerusalem' as he reaches 'the threshing-floor of Ornan the Jebusite' (which will later become the site for the temple), suggests a pestilence or plague moving southwards through Israel towards Jerusalem and Judah but halting on the northern edge of David's city.

The god who apparently plans to reside in Jerusalem moves to halt the pestilence before anyone in Jerusalem seems to be aware of their imminent peril. 'Yahweh saw and repented concerning the evil' (v. 15 [NRSV softens matters somewhat by saying that the deity 'relented concerning the calamity']). No Jerusalemites see the destroying angel until some time later, when 'David looked up and saw the angel of Yahweh' (v. 16). Perhaps also 'the elders' who 'fell on their faces' alongside the king are also meant to have seen the angel at that time, although the reader might think of them as following the king's lead without questioning what he believed he was seeing, but one of the significant characters does not see the angel until considerably later ('Ornan turned and saw the angel' only in v. 20, even though it was already standing by Ornan's threshing-floor in v. 15). Thus before David 'sees' (in v. 16) and 'says' (in v. 17) to Yahweh that his 'hand' should be drawn back, Yahweh 'sees' (in v. 15) and 'says' (in the same verse) to his destroying angel that his 'hand' should be drawn back. Perhaps in this story Israel's god does not quite realize the implications of what he is doing until that moment, or does not perceive the full consequences of the 'evil' he had unleashed until Jerusalem is about to be destroyed, but as befits a god he still sees more than mortals see and acts mercifully towards his chosen city, if not towards the 70,000 northerners his angel has already dispatched.

What are known somewhat jocularly in modern times as 'Acts of God' were evidently believed by the ancient Hebrew traditionalists to be precisely that in a very serious sense, and to occur not for reasons of blind Mother Nature but for reasons of a heavenly Authority. The modern mind, presented with a tale concerning a plague following upon the heels of a census, might look for an epidemiological explanation, perhaps speculating that a plague could be spread throughout a country by a king's census-takers travelling from town to town and gathering the inhabitants of each place together in confined spaces in order to take down their details and issue instructions about future payment of taxes or service in the royal army. But in ancient Israelite thinking, a tale concerning a plague following upon the heels of a census is a moral tale about Israel's god repaying evil for evil. 'Is there evil in a city [NRSV 'Does disaster befall a city'], unless Yahweh has done it?', asks the prophet

Amos rhetorically in Amos 3.6. 'I make peace and I create evil' (NRSV 'I make weal and create woe'), boasts Yahweh himself in Isaiah 45.7. If calamity falls upon Yahweh's people, then there was a body of theological opinion which held that it was justified, either by the deity's need to prove his power and glory or more particularly by specific wrongdoing on the part of the nation or the national monarch. In this story there was a certain supposed wrongdoing—though the Annalists cannot seem quite to put their finger on exactly what was wrong—on the part of David, who had issued an 'abhorrent command' (v. 6) which brought 'guilt upon Israel' (v. 3) and 'displeased' Israel's god (v. 7); a certain calamity must follow, as surely as night follows day.

When Yahweh commands his angel to stop, the angel is 'standing by the threshing-floor of Ornan the Jebusite' (v. 15). In an earlier episode the relocation of the sacred ark had come to a halt at 'the threshing-floor of Chidon' (13.9) when Yahweh had become upset over an alleged infringement of the ark's sacredness, and in a later episode certain Israelite plans will come to a halt at 'the threshing-floor at the entrance of the gate of Samaria' (2 Chron. 18.9) when Yahweh misleads a band of assembled prophets by means of a lying spirit, so the Annalists seem to regard threshing-floors as places of consequence in the spiritual scheme of things. The reader might imagine the importance of the movement of the *ruach* ('wind, spirit') at such a venue, or picture a threshing-floor being situated on higher ground, 'between earth and heaven' (v. 16). But the reader might also note that the threshing-floor in this episode is owned by a Jebusite—that Ornan is the owner and not a humble labourer or a mistreated slave is evident insofar as the workplace carries his name (vv. 15, 28) and is purchased from him (vv. 22-25). This is of interest in the wider story of David because in the episodes leading up to this account the Hebrew king was frequently depicted as killing off or enslaving the populations he conquered (Moabites and Edomites in ch. 18, Ammonites in chs. 19–20). The Jebusites, it seems, have been treated more leniently, since at least one of them has been permitted to live and prosper.

When the king sees the angel of Yahweh standing with a drawn sword in his hand (reminiscent of a story told in Numbers 22.31), he falls to the ground and pleads for his people: 'It is I who have sinned and done very wickedly; but these sheep, what have they done?' (v. 17). With some amendment to the traditional Hebrew text in the second phrase (reading a form of the verb *ra'ah*, 'to shepherd', in one instance instead of two forms of the verb *ra'a'*, 'to do evil'), that part of the royal plea can be read as 'and the shepherd has acted wickedly', in which form it makes an attractively poetic contrast to the 'sheep' who have done no wrong, and picks up the imagery of shepherding the people of Israel already encountered in 11.2 and 17.6-7. Now no less than 70,000 of 'these sheep' have died, through no fault of their own. Later, actual sheep—no more culpable than these metaphorical ones—will substitute for further human casualties when the king presents burnt-offerings on a new altar on the site of the threshing-floor (v. 26), and only then does Yahweh instruct his angel to resheathe his sword. It seems that only a great deal of innocent blood will satisfy a deity bent on destruction.

David says the noble thing in v. 17, namely that Yahweh's hand should be against him and against his 'father's house' rather than against the people at large. Perhaps the reader is meant to be startled here and to consider briefly the possibility that David's god might have repented of the promises he had made through Nathan in the earlier episode of ch. 17, and eaten those words of assurance that David's house would be secure. In the world that the Annalists have created it is startling enough that the golden boy David seemed to be so easily led astray from perfect obedience to the divine will into this apparently displeasing project of taking a census. But our faith in David, and his usefulness as a role-model, is reinstated through this act of contrition, wherein he offers to sacrifice all that he has achieved for himself and his house if only the divine wrath will pass from the people.

In response to David's contrition, the angel of Yahweh commands Gad to tell David what to do next (v. 18). Again the deity does not communicate directly with the monarch, and seems on this occasion not to communicate directly with the seer either, but only to Gad through the mediation of the formerly destroying angel and thence to David through the instructions of the seer. But though the communication channels are complex, the message is clear: Yahweh wants 'an altar to [himself] on the threshing-floor of Ornan the Jebusite' (v. 18), so David immediately sets about providing it; it is certainly an easier price to pay than his life and the lives of his relatives that he had rhetorically offered in v. 17.

At the end of the episode (in 22.1) it will be confirmed that what has been Ornan's threshing-floor is going to become Yahweh's temple, but that is not said at first. In any event Ornan himself does not seem overly impressed with Yahweh's activities and plans, for when he 'turned and saw the angel, and while his four sons who were with him hid themselves, Ornan continued to thresh wheat' (v. 20). Ornan's response to seeing the angel of Yahweh is rather different to that of David when he had seen the angel. Whereas the Israelite king—and each elder with him—had fallen on his face (v. 16), the Jebusite landowner simply continues with the task at hand, although his sons take a less calm view of the situation. Ornan only stops threshing wheat when he sees the king, at which point he does 'obeisance to David with his face to the ground' (v. 21), something he had declined to do before David's god.

When David tells Ornan to 'give me the site of the threshing-floor that I may build on it an altar to Yahweh' (v. 22), the reader's first thought may be of an official confiscation of the Jebusite's land, a simple appropriation of the estate by royal fiat, but the regal character quickly reassures all concerned by saying that he wants it to be given 'at its full price', a magnanimity he demonstrates again—after Ornan has politely declined payment—by insisting, 'No; I will buy them for the full price' (v. 24). The scene is redolent of a haggling match, not unlike a story once told about the ancestor Abraham haggling over the purchase of a burial cave for his family (Genesis 23.3-16). For the Jebusite party the stakes are high: if the king were to take Ornan's offer of everything-for-free literally, he would presumably impoverish the family—and indeed as an all-conquering monarch he has shown himself in earlier episodes to be quite willing simply to take things for himself and for his planned temple (for example, 'from Tibhath and from Cun, cities of Hadadezer, David took a vast quantity of bronze; with it Solomon made the bronze sea and the pillars and the vessels of bronze' [18.8]).

But on this occasion David is generous. He pays his Jebusite subject '600 shekels of gold by weight for the site' (v. 25), an enormous amount. Thus the Annalists signal that nothing is to be cheap about the house of Yahweh, neither in the acquisition of the site itself nor later in the other preparations that must be made for its construction and outfitting. There may even be a further aspect of David undoing some of the damage that had been done by counting the people. Exodus 30.12-14 stipulates that 'When you take a census of the Israelites to register them, at registration all of them shall give a ransom for their lives to Yahweh, so that no plague may come upon them for being registered. This is what each one who is registered shall give: half a shekel...as an offering to Yahweh.' If the Annalists had the legislation of Exodus in mind in telling the story of a plague coming upon the Israelites because of a census, then the 600 shekels that David hands over for the newly designated sacred site may be interpreted as a kind of ransom for the lives of his people. 600 shekels are 1200 half-shekels, representing a hundredfold ransom for each of the twelve tribes of Israel, and perhaps reflecting Joab's reference at the beginning of this episode to a hundredfold increase of Yahweh's people.

To mark the inauguration of this splendid new altar, a now well-pleased Yahweh sends 'fire from heaven onto the altar of burnt-offering' (v. 26). The same offerings mentioned on this occasion—namely 'burnt-offerings and offerings of well-being'—had been offered by David when he had successfully brought the sacred ark into Jerusalem (16.1-2), and so it is only appropriate to have him repeat the exercise now that the permanent site for the ark is being designated, but although Yahweh had presumably been pleased that the ark had then arrived in the city, it is only now on this special plot of land that he 'answers' David with a pyrological endorsement. This special divine approval of having sacrifices made to him on this particular spot will be underlined when Solomon completes the dedication of the temple, whereupon 'fire came down from heaven and consumed the burnt-offering and the sacrifices, and the glory of Yahweh filled the temple' (2 Chron. 7.1). In the exodus traditions of Israel, it was said that 'the appearance of the glory of Yahweh was like a devouring fire on the top of the mountain in the sight of the people of Israel' (Exodus 24.17); nothing less than that will do for the Annalists' tale of the establishment of the Davidic–Solomonic temple.

Readers are not told how many animals Yahweh burns in this first display in front of David. Perhaps we are meant to think in terms of the full complement of 120,000 sheep—a figure representing 10,000 sheep for each of the twelve tribes of Israel—that he consumes in the second display in front of Solomon (2 Chron. 7.5). Or perhaps we might reckon more modestly with a set of 30,000 sheep, standing as proxy for the one-sixteenth of the Judahites who might otherwise have been struck down by the destroying angel in proportion to the carefully executed death toll among the Israelites. But whatever, if any, precise numbers the Annalists may have in the back of their minds, all the humans assembled in the picture might well sigh with relief that their god appears to be signalling his return to an acceptance of such offerings by fire after his erstwhile slaughter of Israelites by pestilence.

To say that the fire from heaven acts as an endorsement of David's offering of animals to the deity at this site should not 'tame' the episode. A god who rains fire from the skies, albeit on this occasion in a focused stream to the newly raised altar, is a god to be held in awe and fear. He can consume mortals by such means when he has a taste for it ('fire from Yahweh' was said to have burnt several people to death in pentateuchal stories such as Leviticus 10.2 and Numbers 16.35), and indeed his character can even be encapsulated in such an image ('Your god Yahweh is a Devouring Fire', according to Deuteronomy 4.24). This kind of god must be constantly appeased, lest he lash out against his devotees. David had previously arranged for an endless stream of animals to be burnt for Yahweh 'regularly, morning and evening, according to all that is written in the law of Yahweh that he commanded Israel' (1 Chron. 16.40), but those arrangements have apparently not been enough to keep the deity in check. A grander edifice will be required, to stand where the angel of Yahweh stood between earth and heaven; perhaps a house especially constructed for Yahweh on that spot, commemorating the resheathing of the heavenly sword before the gates of Jerusalem, might confine the deity's appetite for flesh to the consumption of mute animals in place of further human victims.

The sword that had been poised to strike Jerusalem is finally (in v. 27) put back in its scabbard to await a later day. Perhaps the 'three days' that had been allotted to its present activity (v. 12) have now passed, or perhaps the destructive deity 'repented concerning the evil' (v. 15) before the full period had elapsed. But a sheathed sword is still available for menace; it has not been beaten into a ploughshare. And so the chapter closes (in v. 30) by depicting a David who remains fearful of his god, still 'afraid of the sword of the angel of Yahweh', a description that echoes the fear that had overcome him earlier in 13.12 when Yahweh had struck out against an Israelite at an earlier threshing-floor. Thus even after the heavenly sword has been resheathed it appears that the king is afraid to pass the spot where he had seen it, and he steadfastly refuses to go back north to Gibeon where the tabernacle remains as it was left in 16.39. Solomon will reconvene an assembly at Gibeon (in 2 Chron. 1.3) prior to the completion of the temple in Jerusalem, but David is afraid to do so. Indeed the mighty king who had once ventured far and wide now remains rooted within Jerusalem, and will never set foot outside the city again. His remaining energies will be devoted to organizing the kingdom from his capital, and especially to making elaborate arrangements for the former threshing-floor of Ornan the Jebusite to be transformed into the one and only high place for the Israelite god; to do anything less might be to place himself in danger of unleashing the divine wrath once again.

Certainly the census episode has provided ample reason for a devotee of Yahweh to be afraid, since the dark side of divinity has been disclosed even as the Annalists move us towards a seemingly happy ending. The storytellers use certain turns of phrase to distance the deity from the nastier parts of the action—it is 'a satan/adversary' who sets the chain of events in motion, and it is a 'destroying angel' who slaughters tens of thousands of innocent citizens—but yet they also want to suggest that Yahweh calls the shots and has particular outcomes in view all along. And in good Hebrew storytelling tradition, they let slip that 'the angel of Yahweh' is in effect Yahweh himself. When they set out the tale itself here in ch. 21, they are reasonably circumspect about this mystical matter, simply stating that 'the angel of Yahweh commanded Gad...' (v. 18) without any note that the deity had issued such instructions to his messenger, but with a subsequent note that Gad then spoke 'in the name of Yahweh' (v. 19). But the slippage between angel and deity becomes more noticeable in 2 Chron. 3.1, where the Annalists report that 'Solomon began to build the house of Yahweh in Jerusalem on Mount Moriah, where Yahweh had appeared to his father David, at the place that David had designated, on the threshing-floor of Ornan the Jebusite'. Read in connection with 1 Chron. 21.16, where it was narrated that 'David looked up and saw the angel of Yahweh standing between earth and heaven', the latter passage is very revealing.

Readers familiar with various Genesis stories would not be surprised at this turn of events. After all, Abraham's pregnant slave-girl Hagar encounters 'the angel of Yahweh' at a spring in the wilderness (Genesis 16.7), and the angel speaks as Yahweh: 'I will so greatly multiply your offspring that they cannot be counted for magnitude' (v. 10); after this encounter Hagar 'called the name of Yahweh who spoke to her, "You are El-roi"', a name meaning 'the god who sees me', and the storyteller has her express (in words the later scribes seem to have had some difficulty in transmitting) her wonder that she has seen the One Who Sees. A similar story about Hagar, with similar slippage between angel and deity, is told in Genesis 21.17-19, followed by the infamous story of Abraham being prepared to sacrifice his son Isaac in ch. 22, only to encounter 'the angel of Yahweh' speaking to him as Yahweh: 'You have not withheld your son, your only son, from me' (v. 12); after this encounter 'Abraham called that place "Yahweh-yireh"', a name meaning 'Yahweh sees'—or, with a slight change from the traditional pronunciation, 'Yahweh appears'. An angel also appears in a dream of Jacob (31.11), and announces 'I am the god of Bethel, where you anointed a pillar and made a vow to me' (v. 13, alluding back to an earlier story in 28.11-22 when Yahweh had appeared to Jacob in a dream at Bethel). Thus the tales of Israel's beginnings provided considerable precedent for the Annalists' slippage between 'the angel of Yahweh' and Yahweh himself.

But if the angel in the story of David's tabulation of his troops is in effect the deity in action, and in interaction with humans, then the suspicion might occur to readers that the 'satan' or 'adverse counsellor' who set the whole episode in motion towards its approved culmination in the designation of the temple site was also in effect Yahweh all along, at least in the sense of being an agent or aspect of the divine will. Again, there is pentateuchal precedent for such a contention, since in Numbers 22.22 it is narrated that 'God's anger was kindled because [Balaam] was going [with the officials of Moab], and the angel of Yahweh took his stand in the road as a satan to him' (NRSV 'as his adversary'); and the expression is repeated in v. 32, when the angel of Yahweh informs Balaam, 'I have come out as a satan [NRSV 'as an adversary'], because your way is perverse before me'. It is interesting that the NRSV avoids the word 'satan' in the Numbers passage, so English readers do not see the angel of Yahweh described as a satan in v. 22 and do not hear him describe himself as a satan in v. 32. But that passage is very instructive, because it shows that any of Yahweh's angels can function as a satan, an agent sent to perform a certain adversarial task for the divine purpose (not as an adversary of the deity, but as a loyal agent).

In addition to the opening phrase concerning a satan standing up against Israel, 1 Chronicles 21 contains several references to a divine agent acting against the people, cutting them down with the sword of pestilence and holding that sword drawn over Jerusalem's neck. The Annalists do not formally link these two characters, and may well have in mind an earthly agent in the first case, but that initial antagonist is not the full sum of the adversarial forces employed in achieving the deity's ends in this episode. Indeed the deity himself is in a sense the adversary, at least at the point where David is forced to choose between 'the sword of your [human] enemies' and 'the sword of Yahweh' (v. 12). Does the deity also then stand behind the mysterious agent of the opening verse, working to entice David to a particular undertaking so that the divine purpose may be achieved, just as that same deity will send a 'lying spirit' to entice a later king of Israel (in 2 Chron. 18)? Certainly this particular episode leads directly to the achievement of something dear to the divine heart, when the king declares (in 1 Chron. 22.1), 'Here shall be the house of the god Yahweh, and here the altar of burnt-offering for Israel'. In effect the deity had designated the site, insofar as he determined that 'the sword of Yahweh' should stop at that point and then commanded David to build an altar there, but it will be left to the king to say explicitly that this is the place where the house of Yahweh must stand.

Once again there has been considerable artistry in the telling of the tale, not least in the suggestive contrasts between 'men who drew the sword' and the angel with a 'drawn sword', or the suggestive parallels between a satan 'standing' against Israel and a destroying angel 'standing' before Jerusalem, to say nothing of the neatness of composition in setting forth three choices of punishment, each involving a threefold period of time. But at base this is a disturbing narrative. 70,000 Israelites have died a nasty death, and countless others have been left bereaved and scarred, apparently because the Devouring Fire desired to have a place in Jerusalem where he might indulge his seemingly unquenchable appetite for animal flesh on a grander scale than before. Such are the bare bones of the story the Annalists have told in this section of their Annals. A satanic verse indeed!

1 Chronicles 22–29:
David's Preparation for his Temple

Chapter 22

The last eight chapters of 1 Chronicles are all to do in one way or another with preparations for the temple. One might think of that edifice as Solomon's temple, since it was built in his reign, but in the Annalists' account it is really David's temple. He makes all the preparations, not only for building the complex itself but also for organizing its personnel. He provides almost everything in terms both of the materials for its construction and of the arrangements for the various activities that will characterize its functioning once it has been built. So in these Annals it is very much David's temple.

Indeed ch. 22 begins with David determining where the temple will be: 'This is the house of the god Yahweh and this is the altar of burnt offering for Israel' (22.1). Something of a parallel with the words of Jacob in Genesis 28.17 can be detected here (although it is covered over somewhat in the NRSV's less literal translation of David's words as 'Here shall be…and here…' rather than 'This is…and this is…'). The eponymous ancestor of Israel, fleeing from his homeland, had a particular dream one night and, when he woke up, exclaimed 'How awesome is this place; this is none other than the House of God and this is the gate of heaven'. Thus David's words are an echo of those words. Jacob/Israel was talking about Bethel, a place which appears only twice and inconsequentially in the Annals (1 Chron. 7.28; 2 Chron. 13.19). It may have been the major shrine of the northern kingdom, but for the Annalists the northern kingdom and its shrines are of no significance. It may have been the major shrine for the first Israelites, as its name Bethel ('House of El' or 'House of God') suggests, and as the Genesis legend involving the first Israel implies. But in these Annals it is this shrine that David sets up, on what the Annalists later call Mount Moriah (2 Chron. 3.1), that is the true 'house of the god Yahweh', as David proclaims in 1 Chron. 22.1.

The founding monarch immediately gives orders regarding what should be done in order to make this more properly and fully a house fit for a deity. Here was the spot where the angel of death had stopped on his way toward Jerusalem, the very place where David had seen the angel of Yahweh (21.16). Later it will be reported (in 2 Chron. 3.1) that the king had in fact seen Yahweh himself at that place, so there can be no doubt that this is the correct site for Yahweh's house. Accordingly, David gives orders 'to gather together the aliens who were residing in the land of Israel' (1 Chron. 22.2), that is to say the non-citizens, those who live in this land but do not have the rights and honours that the king's fellow countrymen do. It looks like forced labour here, that non-Israelites are made to build this temple. The Annalists do not say who David gave the instructions to, but one can imagine that the taskmasters are the army. Perhaps the enforcers are that shadowy group mentioned earlier in passing, 'the Cherethites' (18.17), whose title may mean 'the cutters', a designation that could put fear into any slave class. An invidious policy of putting some of the enslaved in charge of enforcing the enslavement, as well as making it explicit in numerical terms that every single one of the disenfranchised are rounded up for the building work, is set out in 2 Chron. 2.17-18: 'Solomon took a census of all the aliens who were residing in the land of Israel, after the census that his father David had taken, and there were found to be 153,600; from these he assigned 70,000 as labourers, 80,000 as stone cutters in the hill country, and 3600 as overseers to make the people work'.

Readers with an awareness of the exodus traditions of ancient Israel cannot help but draw to mind similar language used of the Israelites themselves. The book of Exodus begins by picturing the children of Israel, as resident aliens in the land of Egypt, being given the task of building for the 'new king' of that land (Exodus 1.8), who 'set task-masters over them to oppress them with forced labour; and they built supply cities, Pithom and Rameses, for Pharaoh' (v. 11). We might imagine that part of the building project was the construction of a temple or two for the Egyptian gods. Well, the boot is most certainly on the other foot here in the Annals. The 'new king' in Israel sets the resident aliens to work on a grand building project in the land of Israel, the construction of the temple for the Israelite god. It is forced labour—in effect slave labour—that is used to build it. And the project depends on the wealth that the new king of Israel has forcefully taken from various peoples that he has conquered.

The mention of 'bronze' in 22.3 already reminds readers of an earlier event in 18.8 where David had been seizing bronze from conquered peoples and was stockpiling it for the temple which Solomon would build. That was the first small narrative indication (following the indication of succession in the earlier genealogy) that Solomon would be the one who would succeed David and would in fact build the temple. Now it is more formalized, as Solomon is designated (in 22.5) by his father as the son under whose reign 'the house…is to be built for Yahweh'. The narrative then continues (in v. 6), 'He called for his son Solomon and charged him to build a house for Yahweh, the god of Israel'. Thus a formal passing of the mantle is depicted, though it is unclear who is present at various stages of proceedings. It may be that David's words in v. 5 are meant to be his thoughts to himself in adopting the course of action he fixes upon, and that his words in vv. 7-16 are meant to be his private words to his son without others necessarily being present. But if it is a private word at first, then matters open out to the public sphere in v. 17, where 'David also commanded all the leaders of Israel to help his son Solomon'.

What David reports to Solomon, whether in private or in public, in vv. 8-10 does not exactly correspond with the earlier narrative in ch. 17. The king reports that 'the word of Yahweh came to me', without going into the detail that it had come through the prophet Nathan. Failure to give credit to the prophet is of no particular consequence, other than suggesting that the earlier description of David and Yahweh speaking to each other (14.10, 14) should not be taken as implying a belief on the Annalists' part that no intermediary was involved on those occasions. Of more significance is the different account of the divine message itself. In Nathan's oracle the deity was quoted as saying 'You shall not build me a house to live in, for I have not lived in a house since the day I brought out Israel to this very day' and—to paraphrase a lengthy speech into a short sentence—'I have never asked that a house be built for me' (17.4-6). But in David's words to Solomon the deity is quoted as saying 'You shall not build a house for my name, for you have shed much blood in my sight on the earth' (22.8). This reads rather strangely, because in each of the bloodshedding episodes in these Annals of King David, the warring monarch has had the god of Israel on his side; indeed in a number of places it is that god himself who was the one shedding blood on behalf of his chosen king, giving him victory almost miraculously as though heavenly troops are involved and the earthly troops hardly need to get their swords red at all.

If we are to make sense of this within the Annalists' worldview, then the key is presumably in v. 9, where the royal account of the divine words runs 'a son shall be born to you, and he shall be a man of peace; I will give him peace from all his enemies on every side, for his name shall be Solomon (*shlomo*), and I will give peace (*shalom*) and quiet to Israel in his days'. The basic idea of a son succeeding David had been present in the dynastic oracle of ch. 17, but spelling out that 'he shall be a man of peace' and that 'his name shall be Solomon' are new developments. Solomon was not mentioned by name by Nathan and there was no explicit prophecy about giving 'peace and quiet in his days', though it was implied in the earlier words about how 'I will appoint a place for my people Israel, and will plant them, so that they may live in their own place, and be disturbed no more…and I will subdue all your enemies' (17.9-10). It seems that peace and quiet is required before Yahweh can put his feet up in his house. The god of Israel must be at rest from the wars that he has had to be engaged in to give his people rest, and the people must be at rest so that they can now have the kind of more settled life that includes a fixed temple rather than a portable tent. Thus the highly symbolic name of 'Solomon' ('His Peace'), though it was not mentioned in Nathan's prophecy, might conceivably be taken as having been implied there. In any event, although most of what David says in ch. 22 does not correspond directly with ch. 17's account of the divine words, what he says in 22.10 is certainly in keeping with the earlier oracle: 'He shall build a house for my name; he shall be a son to me, and I will be a father to him, and I will establish his royal throne in Israel forever' (22.10) is rather like 17.12-14.

The first thoughts of the founder of the fledgling dynasty, as he sets up the temple-building project, are that 'my son Solomon is young and inexperienced' (22.5), and he will enunciate exactly the same thoughts again later to the whole assembly (29.1). In his words to the youth in question, he expresses the hope that 'Yahweh [will] grant you discretion and understanding' (22.12), which is very much the kind of thing that Solomon subsequently prays for (in 2 Chron. 1.10) when he succeeds to the throne. Curiously, the Annalists do not give us a figure for Solomon's age at his ascendancy. For his successors, they are generally assiduous on such computations, telling us for example that Solomon's successor Rehoboam 'was 41 years old when he began to reign' (2 Chron. 12.13), the most advanced age of ascendancy of any of the kings in these Annals, with the single though brief exception of Ahaziah at the grand old age of 42 (2 Chron. 22.2). On the lower end of the scale, 'Joash was seven years old when he began to reign' (2 Chron. 24.1), while Josiah and Jehoiachin each had the crown thrust upon them at the age of eight (2 Chron. 34.1 and 36.9 respectively). The average age of coronation in the Annals is actually 22 years of age, so it may be that we are to think of Solomon as considerably younger than that at the time of his own succession to the throne (unless this depiction of the new monarch as 'young and inexperienced' is meant to be an idealistic trope for any newly crowned king no matter what his actual age). Presumably we are not to think of Solomon as being even younger than the particularly juvenile Joash, who was lifted onto the throne at a time of national chaos and ruled for some years under the tutelage of the chief priest (2 Chron. 22–24). Solomon takes the reins of state very competently in these Annals without mention of tutors (note the confidence and speed of matters in 1 Chron. 29.22-25 and 2 Chron. 1.1-6, 14-17). On the other hand the lists of Solomon's older brothers in the genealogical preamble (1 Chron. 3.1-5) and in part in the narrative about David flourishing in Jerusalem (14.4) imply that Solomon was born somewhat later in David's life than a good number of the founding monarch's children, so the talk of the eventual successor being 'young and inexperienced' may have more credence than at first glance. Each of the nine older brothers, from 'the firstborn Amnon' (3.1) through to the son named 'Nathan' (3.5; 14.4), might be expected to be earlier in line to the throne than the tenthborn Solomon, but the Annals provide no narrative information—beyond the note that 'David's sons were the chief officials in the service of the king' (18.17)—about these potential claimants or their respective fates. The Annals speak later of Solomon's great-great-great-grandson Jehoram putting 'all his brothers to the sword, and also some of the officials in Israel' (2 Chron. 21.4), to ensure his own claim to the throne, but no such policy is ascribed to Solomon, the 'man of peace'; his brothers are not seen as rivals for his office, unless some opposition is gently implied in the label of 'young and inexperienced' twice employed by his father.

In speaking of the handover of leadership, David encourages his successor with the words 'Be strong and of good courage; do not be afraid or dismayed' (1 Chron. 22.13). These phrases appear immediately after he has spoken of the need for the new man 'to observe the statutes and the ordinances that Yahweh commanded Moses for Israel', and it so happens that the words of encouragement which then follow echo the words ascribed in Hebrew tradition to Moses himself when he gave charge to his own successor Joshua (Deuteronomy 31.7-8 also reads 'Be strong and of good courage... Do not be afraid or dismayed', with only an alternative negative particle varying the formulation in the latter phrase, though the NRSV inexplicably varies its English translation of two of the verbs). The Annalists have David repeat these expressions in 1 Chron. 28.20, which strengthens the impression that they are in part modelling the passing of the succession from the great founder David to the inheritor of his legacy Solomon on the way that Hebrew tradition depicts the passing of the Mosaic mantle to Joshua.

In v. 14 David speaks of the 'great pains' with which he has provided for the house of Yahweh. Perhaps this is a reference to the blood he has shed, the warfare he felt that he needed to be involved in, and which his god seemed earlier to have approved and supported. He does not mention the great pains of those whose death and slavery have provided the wealth and the labour for the temple. Nonetheless enormous amounts of booty are listed here: '100,000 talents of gold, 1,000,000 talents of silver, and bronze and iron beyond weighing' (v. 14). Such amazing lavishness should achieve the ambition he had set himself in v. 5, where he had stated that 'the house that is to be built for Yahweh must be exceedingly magnificent, famous and glorified throughout all lands'. These sorts of figures represent what a great empire could marshal, fantastical amounts reiterated in v. 16's 'gold, silver, bronze and iron without limit' (as the New Jewish Publication Society translation has it; the NRSV prefers to apply 'without number' to the workers of v. 15). But even though limitless, uncountable, unweighable amounts of metals and materials have been accumulated, still the king urges his son, 'To these you must add more!' (v. 14). This is incredible hyperbole: to what cannot be counted you must add still more. This temple is to be quite extraordinary, like nothing else on earth.

Only now can such a magnificent structure be built, because, as David proclaims with rhetorical flourish to the leaders of Israel, there is now 'peace on every side' and 'the land is subdued' (v. 18). That was a kind of precondition set in the dynastic oracle of ch. 17, where Yahweh had undertaken to 'subdue all your enemies' (17.10). Thus the king is confident that the rest of the oracle can come to fulfilment, namely that his son 'shall build a house for me [Yahweh], and I [ditto] will establish his throne forever' (17.12), and he enjoins the leaders of Israel to 'go and build the sanctuary of the god Yahweh, so that the ark of the covenant of Yahweh and the holy vessels of the deity may be brought into a house built for the name of Yahweh' (22.19). At this time the Annals depict these two things as being in separate locations, the ark in Jerusalem after an exciting account of its being brought into David's city but the tent of the sanctuary and with it the various holy vessels being at Gibeon (16.39); the plan is that these separated things will be brought together.

Chapter 23

Matters are moving towards the end of David's life, with the king now 'old and full of days' (23.1)—though there is quite some narrative to come before the actual end (in 29.28)—so if he is to achieve a smooth transition he must begin it now. Thus it is that 'he made his son Solomon king over Israel' (23.1). We have to assume here a kind of co-regency, with David still seeming to act as king and taking an active interest in organizational matters, but Solomon enthroned now as a kind of apprentice king, becoming prepared to take the full reins of state when necessary. In assembling 'all the leaders of Israel and the priests and the Levites' (23.2), the old king shows a concern to organize things before the new king takes over completely. What is actually on show is the Annalists' concern that everything be seen to stem from David rather than as growing out of later developments.

In order to effect organizational arrangements, 'the Levites, 30 years old and upward, were counted' (v. 3), although later it is twice said that the numbers relate to those 'from 20 years old and upward' (vv. 24, 27). But if there is confusion about the age of maturity for temple service, there is also potential confusion for readers in the seeming discrepancy between this blatant counting of Levites and the episode in ch. 21. There David was pictured as sinning in counting the people of Israel, while Joab prevented the sin from being even more horrendous by not counting the Levites, but here David has the Levites counted and there is no talk about it being sinful. This may seem a curious discrepancy, but it may be that the Annalists are mindful of a tradition (seen in Numbers 1.4 and 3.15) that the Levites are not to be counted among the other Israelites for military purposes but they are to be counted for cultic purposes, for organizing the life of the temple. Here in 1 Chronicles 23 David is undertaking his levitical numbering for precisely such purposes, whereas the purposes in ch. 21 appeared to be more militaristic. A total is given here (in 23.3) of 38,000 Levites, which can be compared to the 8300 Levite warriors who had come to support David in Hebron (12.26-27); now that David is in Jerusalem and coming toward the end of his reign there has been a fivefold increase. Of course it is not necessarily implied that those figures comprise all of the Levites, even though the Annalists seem to indicate that everyone supports David. Presumably not all of the Levites are able to carry arms and be useful to David in a military context. But it is noticeable at several places that they do have a military aspect, which increases the curiousness of ch. 21 insisting that they should be left out of a military census. Nonetheless, if the two sets of figures are taken at face value, then there is a fivefold increase in David's levitical personnel, and that is a bigger increase than for Israel as a whole, which had demonstrated a threefold increase between the two sets of figures in chs. 12 and 21. Of course one might imagine that the Levites in particular ought to fare better than the Israelites in general, if it is the case that as a group they receive a substantial percentage of the wealth of their fellow Israelites (note the arrangements listed in 6.54-81).

David now 'organized them [i.e. the Levites] into divisions' (v. 6). Two aspects are implied here by the Annalists. One is that the descendants of Levi had not been organized in quite this way before this time, not even by 'Moses, the man of God' (v. 14). But another implication is that they are not free to organize themselves, that their arrangements are determined by royal fiat, with royal interests in mind. There is a threefold division (v. 6): Gershonites (vv. 7-11), Kohathites (vv. 12-20), and Merarites (vv. 21-23). Yet within the Kohathites there is a special group of Aaronites: 'Aaron was set apart to consecrate the most holy things, so that he and his sons forever should make offerings before Yahweh, and minister to him and pronounce blessings in his name forever' (v. 13). Not even the descendants of Moses can appropriate these tasks, though they too are Levites (v. 14). It seems that within the 'tribe' of Levites there is a special priestly clan of Aaronites to be distinguished from their fellow tribesmen in general. Those Levites whose birth has placed them outside the inner circle of Aaronites can aspire only to a different role: 'Their duty shall be to assist the descendants of Aaron for the service of the house of Yahweh' (v. 28) in various chores necessary for the smooth functioning of the cultic system, such as cleaning and carrying and measuring and mixing, and performing certain rituals each morning and evening and on weekly and monthly occasions and at the appointed festivals (vv. 28-31). In short, their task is to look after the sanctuary and to 'attend to the descendants of Aaron, their kindred' (v. 32), so that the Aaronites can 'make offerings before Yahweh and minister to him and pronounce blessings in his name forever' (v. 13).

Chapter 24

The organizational activity continues apace, with the king seeing to it that the Aaronites are organized into 24 divisions (24.1-19), so that 'their appointed duties' can be effectively managed (vv. 3, 19). The detail is given that they were all organized by means of 'lots' (v. 5), a selection process that appears again in the assigning of other levitical duties, namely the divisions of assistants to the priests (v. 31), the divisions of singer-musicians (25.8), and the divisions of gatekeepers (26.13). Thus the casting of lots is mentioned several times throughout these chapters as the means of organizing the cultic personnel. In this way an emphasis is made that it is not by the decree of the king but rather by the will of the deity that particular clans are assigned particular responsibilities. If a temple functionary finds that, as a Jakimite, he is in the twelfth division of the priests (24.12), and another finds that, as a Hothirite, he is in the twenty-first division of the singer-musicians (25.28), and yet another finds that, as a Shuppimite, he is a gatekeeper on the western side of the temple complex, 'at the gate of Shallecheth on the ascending road' (26.16), then each of them can be assured that their lot in life has been determined by divine will.

The precise method of the lottery is not disclosed, but it is all carried out under appropriate supervision. We are told concerning the priestly lottery that 'the scribe Shemaiah son of Nethanel, a Levite, recorded [the falling of the lots] in the presence of the king and the officers and Zadok the [high] priest' and other significant personnel (24.6), and that the levitical lots were also cast 'in the presence of King David and Zadok' and others (24.31). The 'officers' are not explicitly listed as being present for the levitical lottery, which might suggest that this was not as significant as the priestly lottery, but interestingly when it comes immediately afterwards to the 'setting apart' of the three divisions of singer-musicians, it is 'David and the officers of the army' who are mentioned as supervising the lottery (25.1), perhaps suggesting a military aspect to the musicianship being organized. Although it is 'the music in the house of Yahweh' that is being provided for (25.6), the association of Yahweh with the battles of Israel may not be entirely absent from the picture.

Chapter 25

David and 'the officers of the army' now set apart certain Levites for particular kinds of service. Notice that it is the king and the military officers who decide who is going to 'prophesy' (v. 1), and they have control not only over who does so but also over how and what they prophesy. The end of v. 2—'Asaph…prophesied under the direction of the king'—is a very revealing comment, reiterated not only in regard to the Asaphites but also in regard to the other two divisions of musical prophets as well in v. 6—'Asaph, Jeduthun, and Heman were under the order of the king'. It is made clear that the Levites are very much under royal command; their jobs depend on them doing what the king wants, and the officers of the army are there to back up the king, should any Levite become a potential problem in this matter.

It is interesting to note not only the role of army and king in overall control of the Levites, but the way in which the Levites themselves control or induce their prophecies. They prophesy 'with lyres, harps, and cymbals' (v. 1). Is this a picture of temple prophets using music in order to produce a prophetic trance, psyching themselves up by means of beat and rhythm to perform the tasks that are set for them? Or do the Annalists have a much tamer picture in mind, of musical personnel proclaiming the tradition and teaching the officially sanctioned doctrine through musical forms? Meanwhile v. 5 mentions 'Heman, the king's seer' as one of the formative Levites who is charged with duties here. One wonders how many 'seers' David had, since Gad is called a 'seer' in 21.9 and Nathan too, although not called a 'seer' as such but rather a 'prophet' (17.1), delivers a 'vision' (17.15)—literally a 'seeing' (in Hebrew a noun from the same verbal root as 'seer' or 'visionary'). In any event the designations 'seer' and 'prophet' appear to be more or less interchangeable, as is seen in this passage (ch. 25) with its talk of 'prophesying' and of a particular 'seer', and there is no shortage of prophets throughout the Annals.

There is perhaps an ironic note in v. 5, or another insight into the way things work in the Annalists' world, in the comment that 'all these were the sons of Heman, the king's seer, according to the divine promise to exalt him; for the deity had given Heman 14 sons and three daughters'. It is important that the eponymous seer should have many sons to inherit the legacy and ensure a flourishing Hemanite family of temple musicians and seers, 'trained in singing to Yahweh' (v. 7). But how is the reader to imagine that this 'divine promise to exalt him' has been communicated? It is presumably the seer Heman himself who has said that the deity has said that this very same Heman is to be exalted. Or perhaps it is someone else among his clan of prophesiers who had said this of him, or it is rather taken as read by the narrators of the tale that some such divine promise must have been made since the blessing of 14 sons is the proof of it. Nevertheless, an image suggests itself of this seer Heman proclaiming that he has seen a rosy future for himself and his progeny—a risky game to play, given that all really depends upon 'the order of the king' and the watchful eyes of 'the officers of the army', but Heman is recorded with honour in the Annalists' levitical lists, so the seer saw well.

In listing the levitical lots, the Annalists wax rhythmically, in an almost musical repetition, from v. 10 onwards: 'the third to Zaccur, his sons and his brothers, twelve; the fourth to Izri, his sons and his brothers, twelve; the fifth to Nethaniah, his sons and his brothers, twelve', and so forth down to 'the twenty-fourth to Romamti-ezer, his sons and his brothers, twelve'. That kind of refrain may remind readers of certain techniques in the psalmic traditions of Israel, such as is seen in Psalm 118.2-4 in brief compass or in Psalm 136.1-26 with even greater persistence than that mustered by the Annalists (in both those psalms the repeated phrase in each verse is 'his steadfast love endures forever'). A background beat of 'his sons and his brothers, twelve' may not appeal to all poetical tastes, but it certainly drives home the message that all is in good order, fully consistent and perfectly balanced, in the levitical arrangements.

Chapter 26

The 'divisions of the gatekeepers' (26.1) are now listed, 'guard corresponding to guard' (v. 16). In the Annalists' world it is presumably vital that ordinary folk should be kept from entering a sacred space that their unconsecrated presence would defile, and so gatekeepers divinely ordained for the purpose of ensuring the uncompromised sanctity of the temple complex are brought forward for such duties. But it is not simply a matter of barring the gates of the holy enclosure against non-sacred persons; these guards have control over 'the storehouse' (vv. 15, 17) and 'the treasuries' (vv. 20, 22, 24, 26). The temple complex is a place of considerable wealth, not least because of all 'the dedicated gifts that King David, and the heads of families, and the officers...and the commanders of the army, had dedicated' (v. 26), much of it 'from booty won in battles' (v. 27). The latter admission that much of Yahweh's personal wealth, or that is to say the bounty enjoyed by the priests and Levites, depends upon war-gotten gains, is a disturbing one, but the need in such circumstances for vigilance on the part of the Levites in guarding their precincts is clear. It is probably also rather prudent that the system is arranged so that 'guard corresponded to guard' (v. 16) and there are always at least 'two and two' on duty at each point (v. 17), lest any individual be provided with an opportunity to make some use of the treasuries that had not been sanctioned by the 'chief officer in charge of the treasuries' (v. 24).

The officials in charge of these precincts have considerable power in the Annalists' temple-centred state. Verse 6 describes certain of those 'who exercised authority' as *gibborey chayil*, which NRSV renders here as 'men of great ability' but which more literally translates as 'warriors of valour' (or 'mighty warriors', as NRSV renders the expression in 12.8). This terminology, with its militaristic flavour, suggests an elite force of fully armed and stolidly determined guardians; these are not simply men with an ability to organize and implement an appropriate sequence of opening and shutting gates or moving important items around a complex site, but a kind of paramilitary force 'set apart' by 'David and the commanders of the army' (as is said of their colleagues in 25.1). Such a view of these Levites is supported by the earlier episode in which more than 4000 Levite warriors rallied to support David in his claim for kingship (12.26) and now in the present passage by that telling phrase of 'booty won in battle' (26.27), including 'all that of Samuel the seer' along with that of various non-levitical military commanders (v. 28). That the Annalists think of Samuel as a Levite is made clear in the opening genealogical listings (assuming that the Samuel of 6.28, 33-38, is intended as the same man as the one referred to in 9.22 and 11.3), so listing him here as a booty-winning commander to rank with 'Saul son of Kish and Abner son of Ner and Joab son of Zeruiah' (26.28) ties the levitical brotherhood very firmly into military involvements.

The close linking of 'the work of Yahweh' and 'the service of the king' in v. 30, reiterated just two verses later in the interweaving of 'everything pertaining to God' and 'the affairs of the king' in v. 32, is instructive about the ideology put forward by the Annalists. Working for the king is working for the deity; loyalty to Yahweh demands loyalty to David and his heirs and successors. And as the reader moves into ch. 27, the matter becomes even more oppressive, with a continuation of detail about the organization of people in charge of the national wealth and access to royal privilege.

Chapter 27

There now begins a list of various persons 'who served the king in all matters concerning the divisions that came and went, month after month throughout the year, each division numbering twenty-four thousand' (27.1)—which leads into another hymnic-style refrain (similar to what was seen in 25.9-31), 'and in his division were twenty-four thousand' (vv. 2, 4, 5, 7-15). This twelvefold repetition that there are an equal number of highly trained and strongly armed military personnel on duty 'month after month throughout the year' drives home the point that the king's army is organized for constant alertness. If they are on the alert against non-Israelite enemies that might revolt against the Israelite imperialism in which David seems to be engaged (judging by the conquests and enslavements listed in earlier chapters), then Israelites at least might relax, though those 'enemies' might feel all the more aggrieved at being so systematically held under David's bondage. But are the Annalists equally depicting the Israelite people themselves being kept under control? In v. 16 onwards, various commanders are set 'over the tribes of Israel', with apparently each tribe assigned such an official. Thus all 12 months are covered (vv. 1-15) and then all 12 tribes are covered (vv. 16-22, though the twelvefold division here does not exactly correspond to that encountered elsewhere in the Annals). It seems that there is no place, as well as no time, in which the king's control can be avoided.

At the end of the chapter (vv. 25-31) we have some account of the royal dominance of the economy. The king has 'treasuries in the country, in the cities, in the villages, and in the towers' (v. 25), and he has over-seers 'over those who did the work of the field' (v. 26), 'over the vineyards' and their produce (v. 27), 'over the olive and sycamore trees' and 'the stores of oil' (v. 28), 'over the herds that pastured in Sharon' and 'the herds in the valleys' (v. 29), and 'over the camels', 'the donkeys' and 'the flocks' (v. 30); all of this is 'King David's property' (v. 31). It seems as if nothing is free of the king's control, that all of the nation's wealth flows into the royal coffers. The hand of the monarch stretches over the whole land and its people. It is as though David has appropriated all of Israel during his 40-year reign, that he has fashioned a nation which serves only him—and the centralized temple state that he is organizing.

In the midst of this account of the king's total control of the nation, there is a reference (in 27.23-24) to what had been narrated in ch. 21, namely the 'wrath' that 'came upon Israel' for David's counting of the Israelites, and a hint is given as to why the deity may have become wrathful over the incident: 'David did not count those below 20 years of age, for Yahweh had promised to make Israel as numerous as the stars of heaven'. Given this divine promise, is it a mark of unfaithfulness to count the Israelites and see how numerous they were? Perhaps one should not be able to count them all, on account of their sheer numerousness, just as one cannot count the stars of heaven (as Yahweh implies to Abraham in Genesis 15.5).

Another interesting sidelight may be seen at the end of v. 24, where reference is made to 'the Annals of King David', or in Hebrew *divrey hayyamim lammelek david*. The book of Chronicles itself is known in Hebrew tradition as *divrey hayyamim*, 'the Annals' or 'the Chronicles'. In a sense we have in 27.24 a name that could be applied to the book of 1 Chronicles, were it to be regarded as a stand-alone entity: the annals of King David. Obviously, however, their own book (or rather portion of a book) is not the work that the Annalists are referring to here; they rather want their readers to think that there was an account made of David's reign during the time of that reign, and thereby to be reassured that the Annalists' own work is based upon sure and reliable sources (such as also 'the records of the seer Samuel' and other records mentioned in 29.29).

Note is made again (in 27.34, as it was in 18.15) that Joab is commander of the king's army. We have come full circle, and we see again that the army is the main player that keeps all of this system in line. There are 'counsellors', there are 'scribes', there is even 'the king's friend' (vv. 32-33)—the latter presumably a title of honour for a close associate or high courtier—just as various important officials have similarly been listed earlier (18.15-17), but underlining everything is 'the king's army' and its 'commander', so it is that man who receives the ultimate position (namely 27.34) in the listing of David's men.

Chapter 28

All appropriate pomp and circumstance is now marshalled for the occasion of David passing his royal mantle publicly to Solomon (28.1). The Annalists like to involve all the people in the significant events of the nation's life—one might compare 'in the sight of all Israel' in v. 8 with 'all Israel' in, for example, 11.10 (when David himself became king) and 2 Chron. 30.5 (when Hezekiah issues a Passover proclamation). David is now depicted (in vv. 2-10) as telling everyone what he had previously told Solomon in the earlier speech of 22.7-16. That the king 'rose to his feet' indicates the formal occasion of the speech, and the first words,

'Hear me', will turn out to be a typical opening for royal speeches in the Annals as a whole (as in 2 Chron. 13.4; 20.20; 29.5).

On this occasion the reason given for why David is only making preparations for the temple and will not actually be building it is that a divine word had decreed, 'You shall not build a house for my name, for you are a warrior and have shed blood' (28.3). David had been too busy fighting and establishing the kingdom (compare 22.8—although 17.1-6 had suggested that Yahweh did not want a house at first). Apparently the shedding of blood is taken as constituting a certain ritual uncleanness rather than an ethical fault, since the Annals have plenty of good words to say about shedding the blood of Israel's enemies. 'Warrior' is literally 'a man of wars/battles' (*ish milchamot*), to be contrasted with the 'man of peace/rest' (*ish menucha*) in 22.9 (and the 'house of rest' [*bet menucha*] here in 28.2).

The royal speech sets out concentric circles of increasingly specific selection, culminating first in David (v. 4) and then in Solomon (v. 5) as the men chosen by their god, reflecting in a nutshell the detailed genealogies of chs. 1–9. (So too there are concentric circles of holiness in the description of the temple plan within v. 11 and then in vv. 12-18, culminating each time in the place where the deity had chosen to centre himself.) A divine undertaking is made that Solomon's kingdom will be established 'forever' (v. 7), though that possibility is offset against the possibility of being abandoned 'forever' (v. 9). Those latter royal words, 'If you seek him'—i.e. 'your father's god…Yahweh'—'he will be found by you, but if you forsake him, he will abandon you forever', are something of a summary of the Annalists' theology (note also 1 Chron. 10.13-14 and 2 Chron. 15.2); this 'seeking' or 'abandoning' Yahweh will become an important concept for their presentation of the post-Solomonic kings, and presumably a central theme which they would wish their readers to note. In the event, the Annals will tell (in 2 Chron. 1–9) of a Solomon who indeed 'continues resolute in keeping my [i.e. Yahweh's] commandments and my ordinances, as he is today' (v. 7), yet they will also tell (in 2 Chron. 36) of the end of that kingdom and of its possible new beginning.

The exhortations are at first in the plural (v. 8's '*observe* and *search out* all the commandments of *your* god Yahweh, that *you may possess* this good land, and *leave* it for an inheritance to *your* children forever'), so they are addressed to all those who had assembled in v. 2, before words are then directed to the singular Solomon in v. 9 to 'know' and 'serve' and 'seek'. The chosen one is then exhorted to 'be strong, and act' (v. 10). In Israelite tradition Moses was represented as having given similar words of encouragement to Joshua (the formulations to be seen in Deuteronomy 31.7-8 are reflected more precisely in David's further exhortation to Solomon here in v. 20: 'be strong and bold', 'do not be afraid or dismayed', and 'he will not fail you or forsake you'); Joshua's task in those other tales was to step across the threshold of the Jordan, while Solomon's task in this tale is to set up the threshold of the temple.

The orderly transition from David to Solomon includes the handing over of the temple 'plan'. This word, which is used twice at the beginning (vv. 11, 12) and twice at the end (vv. 18, 19) of the description of these plans, is the same word as is used with reference to the plans for the tabernacle in Exodus 25.9, 40 (though NRSV translates the word as 'pattern' in Exodus), and there is much in common between the basic plans of tabernacle and temple. The reader familiar with the exodus traditions is thus assured that in the setting of Israel's worship life there is a firm continuity from Moses to David and Solomon (a point to be reiterated in 2 Chron. 5.5), and by implication also to the re-establishment of the temple after the exile. The plan itself is probably to be thought of as a description in words of the dimensions, materials and furnishings of the complex rather than a drawing. Here in v. 11 the introductory description culminates in 'the room for the mercy seat', a chamber otherwise known as 'the holy of holies' or the most sacred inner place of the temple complex. The fuller description of vv. 12-18, after picturing the surrounding chambers and their appointments, likewise culminates in v. 18 in this innermost room, with a reference to the covering for the sacred ark. In this way the Annalists suggest concentric circles of graduated holiness focusing on the spot where the deity had chosen to centre himself, just as the concentric circles of the genealogies, as re-expressed in vv. 4-5, focused on the individual who had been divinely chosen. The word here translated 'the mercy seat' could be translated 'the cover' (as the NRSV footnote suggests) and is related to the word for 'making atonement': it refers to the gold covering-slab of the ark which functioned in the atonement ritual (Leviticus 16.11-16).

The Annalists virtually break out into song as they describe the temple plans. There are rhythmical repetitions of a number of phrases, such as the repeated 'service in the house of Yahweh' in v. 13, the repeated 'vessels for each service' in v. 14, and the repeated 'lampstand and its lamps' in v. 15. The word 'all' in the Hebrew occurs like an insistent chime throughout the passage, seven times in vv. 12-14 alone, emphasizing that absolutely everything connected with the temple was ordained in the plan which David gave to Solomon. 'In mind' (v. 12) is literally 'in (or 'by') the spirit', an expression which might suggest—particularly in the context of what is said in v. 19—that the temple plans came to the king under divine inspiration; but it might simply denote mental activity, as it does in Ezekiel 11.5 ('the things that come into your mind'). 'All the vessels' (v. 13) again recalls Exodus 25.9 (where NRSV translates 'all its furniture'); when the expression is used once more in 2 Chron. 36.18, it may reflect a hope by the Annalists that all could be returned to Jerusalem for a rebuilt temple.

The Annalists perhaps imply in v. 19 that they were able to consult a written record from David's time setting out the temple plan. They might also be suggesting, through the expression 'at Yahweh's direction' (literally, 'from the hand of Yahweh'), that the deity himself had inscribed it, as Exodus 31.18 says of the tablets of the law—although 'the hand of Yahweh' might simply refer to divine inspiration. The all-important little word 'all' is repeated twice in this verse, to emphasize once again that absolutely everything connected with the temple stems from the divine sphere, and does not arise from human inventiveness or innovation.

Chapter 29

After fully commissioning his successor, David speaks again to the whole assembly (29.1). Since in 28.1 he had assembled all the 'officials', 'officers', 'commanders', 'stewards', and 'warriors', and addressed them, it may be that this further address (29.1-5) is also directed at the same assemblage. At least it is the 'leaders', 'commanders', and 'officers' who respond to the king's words (v. 6), but 'the people' are mentioned (in v. 9) as rejoicing at the response which those functionaries make to the king's address, so it may be that the Annalists imagine a much larger assembly than simply the ruling classes and the military being present for this grand occasion (just as in 28.8 the king had charged his addressees 'in the sight of all Israel').

In this brief address David repeats the idea that Solomon is 'young and inexperienced' (29.1), a view he had expressed perhaps less publicly on an earlier occasion when he had resolved to make preparations for the temple by providing materials in great quantity (22.5). Having fulfilled that resolution, he is now able to report that he has provided all that is necessary for carrying out the building programme: 'gold for gold, silver for silver, bronze for bronze, iron for iron, wood for wood', and various kinds of stone (29.2). In addition to all that provision for the temple project, the king's last will and testament reads, in relation to his further 'personal treasure of gold and silver': 'I give it to the house of my god' (v. 3). Some might regard such a gesture as the deathbed generosity of a monarch who has accumulated the national wealth during his reign but who cannot now take it with him, but the Annalists have not pictured a king who spent his years on the throne wallowing in wealth for its own sake. He is seen to have been hoarding precious materials for a grand purpose of which his chroniclers approve. They do not offer their readers any reaction from the heir Solomon when David's testament gives his potential inheritance away to the temple, but since Solomon will proceed to build the temple with gusto, he must be assumed to be at ease about the situation, and his devotion to the project will bring its own rewards in excess of anything he might have inherited from his father. Indeed 2 Chron. 9.22-24 will claim that Solomon's personal fortune exceeds not only that previously accumulated by his father David but also exceeds that of any other king in the known world (a matter already foreshadowed here in 1 Chron. 29.25), so he will not lose out by David being generous to the temple project.

And certainly the temple project is now left in excellent shape, as David had resolved to do 'before his death' (22.5). He sets out the challenge—or issues an implied command—'Who then will offer willingly?' (29.5), and the temple coffers fill with the 'freewill offerings' of the privileged classes (vv. 6-8) and perhaps also of the people at large, who in any event rejoice with the king at the success of his exhortation to generosity in support of the planned temple. In fashioning this account, the Annalists may have had in mind the story in Exodus 35.4-9 of Moses commanding the Israelites to be generous in giving their gold and silver and precious possessions for the tabernacle project, but in any event the temple project outshines any other undertaking in these Annals, and David's work in making preparation for its construction and furnishing is now done.

A highly satisfied David leads the people of Israel in blessing their god, whose temple is now on the cusp of coming into being. First the king himself pronounces, 'Blessed are you, O Yahweh, god of our ancestor Israel' (29.10), and then he calls upon the whole assembly, 'Bless your god Yahweh' (v. 20). The whole assembly does so, 'prostrating themselves before Yahweh and the king' (v. 20), an association between deity and monarch already set out in the dynastic oracle of ch. 17 but here reinforced by the retiring monarch's words 'yours is the kingdom, O Yahweh' (29.11) and even more so by the narrative moving on to inform us that 'then Solomon sat on the throne of Yahweh, succeeding his father David as king' (v. 23).

The Annalists' accounting will continue with the reign of Solomon and his successors in what we call '2 Chronicles', but the section of their work that might be called the Annals of King David comes to an end with a closing formulation: 'Thus David son of Jesse had reigned over all Israel' (v. 26); he had reigned for 40 years (v. 27), 'and he died in a good old age, full of days, riches, and honour' (v. 28), as befits the hero that has been presented in these Annals. Other accounts of the great man's life and work are claimed to be available—indeed that all 'the acts of King David, from first to last, are written in the records of the seer Samuel, and in the records of the prophet Nathan, and in the records of the seer Gad, with accounts of all his rule and his might and of the events that befell him and Israel and all the kingdoms of the earth' (vv. 29-30)—but from the Annalists' point of view all that we need to know about this primary king of Israel is 'written in the records' that we call '1 Chronicles'. In that 'account of his rule and his might and of the events that befell him and Israel', he is the man who establishes Yahweh's kingdom on earth and who prepares the ground for Yahweh's temple. His first words (in 11.6) had been an exhortation to the Israelites to seize Jerusalem, and his last words (in 29.20) are an exhortation to the Israelites to 'bless your god Yahweh'. On this telling, then, all 'the acts of King David, from first to last', are devoted to the glory of Israel's god through the founding of a political and religious system that sweeps all before it. As 1 Chronicles ends, note should be taken by 'all the kingdoms of the earth'.

Bibliography

Readers seeking further (or alternative) comments on the books of Chronicles may wish to consult the following commentaries:

Braun, R., *1 Chronicles* (Word Biblical Commentary, 14; Waco, TX: Word Books, 1986).

Coggins, R.J., *The First and Second Books of the Chronicles* (Cambridge Bible Commentary; Cambridge: Cambridge University Press, 1976).

Curtis, E., and A. Madsen, *A Critical and Exegetical Commentary on the Books of Chronicles* (International Critical Commentary; Edinburgh: T. & T. Clark, 1910).

DeVries, S.J., *1 and 2 Chronicles* (Forms of Old Testament Literature; Grand Rapids: Eerdmans, 1989).

Dillard, R.B., *2 Chronicles* (Word Biblical Commentary, 15; Waco, TX: Word Books, 1987).

Japhet, S., *I & II Chronicles: A Commentary* (Old Testament Library; London: SCM Press, 1993).

McConville, J.G., *I & II Chronicles* (Daily Study Bible; Philadelphia: Westminster Press, 1984).

Myers, J.M., *I Chronicles* and *II Chronicles* (Anchor Bible, 12 & 13; New York: Doubleday, 1965).

Selman, M.J., *1 Chronicles* and *2 Chronicles* (Tyndale Old Testament Commentaries; Leicester: Inter-Varsity Press, 1994).

Tuell, S.S., *First and Second Chronicles* (Interpretation; Louisville, KY: John Knox Press, 2001).

Wilcock, M., *The Message of Chronicles* (The Bible Speaks Today; Downers Grove, IL: Inter-Varsity Press, 1987).

Williamson, H.G.M., *1 and 2 Chronicles* (New Century Bible Commentary; London: Marshall, Morgan & Scott, 1982).

Several studies on various aspects of the interpretation of Chronicles may also be of interest:

Ackroyd, P.A., *The Chronicler in his Age* (JSOTSup, 101; Sheffield: JSOT Press, 1991).

Auld, A.G., *Kings Without Privilege: David and Moses in the Story of the Bible's Kings* (Edinburgh: T. & T. Clark, 1994).

Dyck, J.E., *The Theocratic Ideology of the Chronicler* (Biblical Interpretation Series, 33; Leiden: E.J. Brill, 1998).

Japhet, S., *The Ideology of the Book of Chronicles and its Place in Biblical Thought* (Beiträge zur Erforschung des Alten Testaments und des Antiken Judentums, 9; Frankfurt: Peter Lang, 1989; rev. edn, 1997).

Jones, G.H., *1 & 2 Chronicles* (Old Testament Guides; Sheffield: JSOT Press, 1993).

Welch, A.C., *The Work of the Chronicler: Its Purpose and Date* (Oxford: Oxford University Press, 1939).

Williamson, H.G.M., *Israel in the Books of Chronicles* (Cambridge: Cambridge University Press, 1977).

A number of volumes in the *Journal for the Study of the Old Testament* Supplement Series (published by Sheffield Academic Press) deal with angles on the interpretation of Chronicles. In volume-number order, these are:

50. Noth, M., *The Chronicler's History* (1987).
88. Duke, R.K., *The Persuasive Appeal of the Chronicler: A Rhetorical Analysis* (1990).
156. Kleinig, J.W., *The Lord's Song: The Basis, Function and Significance of Choral Music in Chronicles* (1993).
160. Riley, W., *King and Cultus in Chronicles: Worship and the Reinterpretation of History* (1993).
211. Kelly, B.E., *Retribution and Eschatology in Chronicles* (1996).
238. Graham, M.P., K.G. Hoglund and S.L. McKenzie (eds.), *The Chronicler as Historian* (1997).
253. Johnstone, W., *1 and 2 Chronicles, I: 1 Chronicles 1–2 Chronicles 9. Israel's Place among the Nations* (1997).
254. Johnstone, W., *1 and 2 Chronicles, II: 2 Chronicles 10–36. Guilt and Atonement* (1997).
263. Graham, M.P., and S.L. McKenzie (eds.), *The Chronicler as Author: Studies in Text and Texture* (1999).
275. Johnstone, W., *Chronicles and Exodus: An Analogy and its Application* (1998).

Those readers looking for more may wish to consult the following resources and follow the leads to be found there:

Kalimi, I., *The Books of Chronicles: A Classified Bibliography* (Simor Bible Bibliographies; Jerusalem: Simor, 1990).
Kleinig, J.W., 'Recent Research in Chronicles', *Currents in Research: Biblical Studies* 2 (1994), pp. 43-76.

Index of References